Prague

and its environs

First edition, May 1991

I.S.B.N.
English   9963-578-54-3
German   9963-578-55-1
Italian   9963-578-56-x
French   9963-578-57-8

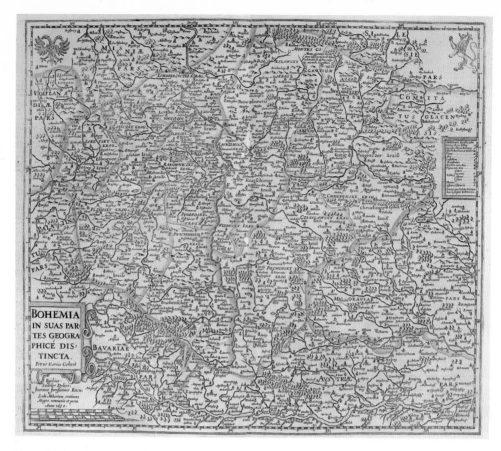

Map of Bohemia engraved in 1630.

CZECHOSLOVAKIA - INTRODUCTION

Situated in the centre of Europe, Czechoslovakia is a landlocked country bordered by Poland to the north, the Soviet Union to the east, Austria and Hungary to the south, and Germany to the west.

The area of the country is 128,000 square kms, stretching 767 kms from east to west and 240 kms from north to south at its widest point.

Czechoslovakia is a federative republic composed of two states, the Czech and Slovak. Its population is 15.6 million with a density of 122 people per square kilometre. The capital, Prague, (1.2 million) is the only city in the country with a population of more than one million.

The second largest city, Bratislava, with a population of 435,000, is the capital of Slovakia. Built on the banks of the Danube, Bratislava has a rich historical and cultural heritage, and is also an important industrial town. The first university in the town was founded in 1465.

Another major town is Brno with a population of 385,000. Settled by the Slavs in the 5th century AD, Brno is the largest city in Moravia and holds an important position in the Czechoslovak economy.

Other towns with a population of more than 100,000 are Ostrava (328,000), Košice (232,000), Pilsen (175,000), Olomouc (106,000), Ústí Nad Labem (105,000), and Liberec (103,000).

Historically the country is divided into three regions. In the northwest are the Czech Lands of Bohemia and Moravia with 10.3 million inhabitants. In the southeast is the Slovak-speaking republic of Slovakia with 5.3 million people.

Bohemia takes its name from the Celtic Boii tribe which lived in the area before the arrival of the Germanic tribes in the eighth century BC. The word Moravia comes from the Morava river.

Czechoslovakia is predominantly Roman Catholic, but there is also a strong Protestant congregation.

Its official languages are Czech and Slovak which despite their differences are mutually understandable and belong to the western Slavonic language group.

Although basically hilly, there are considerable variations in the country's landscape. Bohemia in the west, is enclosed by four mountain ranges, namely the Krušné Hory (Ore mountains) in the northwest, the Krkonoše (Giant Mountains) in the northeast, the Česká Vysočina (Moravian Hills) in the southeast, and the Český Les and Šumava (Bohemian Forest) in the southwest.

Moravia, essentially a lowland area, separates Bohemia from the Carpathian mountains of Slovakia, creating a corridor known at its narrowest as the Moravian Gate.

Slovakia is mountainous with plains and deep valleys dominated by the High and Low Tatras (Vysoké and Nizké Tatry). The highest elevation in the country is Gerlach peak (Gerlachovský štít) in the High Tatras (2,655 m).

Czechoslovakia has a number of important rivers which together with their tributaries stretch tens of thousands of kilometres. The longest, the Vltava (more than 400 km), a tributary of the Elbe (Labe), flows through Prague. Another important river is the Váh (390 km).

The only rivers which are truly navigable are the Elbe, the Vltava and the Danube. The Danube makes a slight inroad into Czechoslovakia before forming part of the border with Hungary. Its significance as a thoroughfare for trade has made Bratislava an important port.

The country also has a multitude of lakes, most of them of glacial origin, and more than 3,000 mineral and thermal springs. These have led to the establishment of several well known spa towns, the best known of which

A 19th century engraving of the High Tatras.

is Karlovy Vary (Karlsbad). One third of the country is forested.

The climate is continental with an average temperature of 9 C. There are four characteristic seasons although there are climatic variations within the various regions of the country. Spring and autumn are changeable, while the winter is cold and the summer hot. During the summer temperatures rise to more than 19 C while in the winter they fall to around freezing point.

More than 50 per cent of the land is agricultural. Major crops include wheat and spelt, barley, sugar beet and potatoes. Pigs, cattle, sheep and chickens are bred, while the fishing sector, dominated by carp, is important.

The most important minerals are brown and hard coal. Czechoslovakia was one of the first Central European countries to experience the industrial revolution and manufacturing and mining continue to form the backbone of the economy. Although the country has developed metallurgy, engineering, chemical, automobile and arms industries, it is its

Detail of the exterior of a house in Prague.

porcelain and glass products that are best known abroad. Bohemian crystal is appreciated and sought after the world over.

Czechoslovakia is also well-known for its tradition in brewing. One brewery, U Fleků, has been producing dark beer since 1499. Its best known beers are Pilsner and Budvar (Budweiser). Pilsner beer has been brewed since the 13th century and takes its name from the town of Plzeň (Pilsen) where it originates. The name is now used by brewers everywhere to describe light lager beers. Good quality hops and the purity of the water have established an international reputation for Czechoslovakian beer.

Although basically a beer-drinking country, Czechoslovakia also has some very good local wines. Vines are believed to have been imported from Burgundy in the 14th century by Charles IV and the tradition has flourished although the country's wines are little-known abroad. Czechs also produce liqueurs. The best known among them are the plum liqueur slivovice and the juniper liqueur borovička.

Czechoslovakian cuisine is hearty and rather heavy. Thick soups, roast pork or fillet of beef with cream sauce, roast goose for special occasions, served with dumplings (houskové or bramborové knedlíky) of all shapes and sizes is the traditional fare. Lots of hot sweet fritters such as dalken filled with plum jam, and palatchinken (crepes), filled with apricot jam, are typical desserts. But the most popular dessert of all is sweet fruit dumplings (ovocné knedlíky). Prague is also the birthplace of the now world famous frankfurter, available at street corners and in restaurants.

The country boasts a long and rich musical tradition due in part to the long-standing inclusion of music lessons in the school curriculum. From 1800 on, school children have been taught to play a musical instrument of their choice and most orchestras abroad feature at least one Czech musician in their ranks.

In the past Prague regularly played host to some of the world's greatest composers. They include Wolfgang Amadeus Mozart, whose Don Giovanni was premiered at the Tyl theatre in 1787, Niccolo Paganini, Franz Liszt, Richard Wagner, Gustav Mahler and Hector Berlioz. Unlike other European countries, music was performed not only for the aristocracy but in public theatres frequented by the middle classes.

Czechoslovakia did not just welcome visiting composers, but can claim to have given the world some of the most acclaimed musicians of all time. Top of the list are Bedřich Smetana (1824-1884), who established a national musical style especially for opera, Antonín Dvořak (1841-1904), best known for his orchestral works, notably the New World Symphony, and Leoš Janáček (1854-1928) known for his operas.

Music can be enjoyed at the world famous Prague Spring Festival in May and June and the Bratislava Music Festival in September, as well as in concert halls throughout the year.

Czechoslovakia, a book-loving country, has produced many important writers, and it is perhaps no coincidence that after the Velvet Revolution its first elected president was the world acclaimed playwright Václav Havel.

Perhaps its best known author is Franz Kafka (1883-1924), whose works "The Trial" and "The Castle" are acknowledged masterpieces.

Other famous writers are Jaroslav Hašek (1883-1923), known for his best-seller "The Good Soldier Schweik", and poet Jaroslav Seifert (1910-1986) awarded the Nobel Prize for literature in 1984.

Czechoslovakia's rich history is amply illustrated by its more than 2,000 castles and monumental cities. These combine with the lush scenery, impressive cultural scene and hospitable and courteous people to make the country a choice destination for all.

CZECHOSLOVAKIA - HISTORICAL SURVEY

Detail of the exterior of a house in Prague.

The state of Czechoslovakia was proclaimed on October 28, 1918, following the break-up of the Austro-Hungarian Empire at the end of World War I. It represented the culmination of efforts by the Czechs and the Slovaks to form a single state.

Czechs and Slovaks settled in the area around the fifth century and lived together until the 10th century. Their paths separated after the Magyars conquered the Carpathian basin. Slovakia was incorporated into historic Hungary, while the Czechs maintained the Kingdom of Bohemia. Even though both Czechs and Slovaks later formed part of the Austro-Hungarian Empire their fate at the hands of the Habsburgs differed sharply: Moravia and Bohemia prospered as industrialised areas while Slovakia remained essentially agricultural. Having lived next to each other for close to 1,000 years the two chose to unite in 1918.

The area has been continuously settled from the dawn of civilisation. From 400 BC to 100 AD the Celts built a strong network of fortresses (oppids), developed handicrafts and minted their own coins. The Celts were expelled by the German Marcomans and Kvades tribes who continuously waged war against the Roman Empire. The first Slav tribes came to Bohemia at around the fifth century. The most powerful among them were the Čechové (Czechs) who came to rule the area. The Slav tribes were conquered by the Avars, but later they united under Merchant Samon and overthrew them in the early seventh century.

Economic growth encouraged political development and in the ninth century the Slav tribes were organised into a political unit known as the Great Moravian Empire. The Empire fought with varying success against the East Frankish Empire, relying on help from Byzantium, but succumbed to the Magyars in the early 10th century. Its defeat resulted in the different destinies of western and eastern Czechoslovakia. After the collapse of Great Moravia the western part flourished as the Kingdom of Bohemia, while the eastern part, inhabited by Slovaks, was annexed by Hungary. It was only after 1,000 years that the Czechs and Slovaks were able to establish their own, united state.

THE CZECHS

The Kingdom of Bohemia came into being in the 10th century under the House of Přemyslid which held power until 1306. Converted to Christianity, the rulers of the House of Přemyslid were instrumental in spreading Christianity and offered the country several saints, among them St. Wenceslas, patron saint of Bohemia.

The first Prague bishopric and the first churches were founded in the 10th century. But the ties between Bohemia and the Holy Roman Empire were strained as the Holy Roman Emperors attempted to intervene in the internal affairs of Bohemia.

King Přemysl Otakar I (1197-1230) managed, through skilful diplomacy, to acquire the Golden Bull of Sicily in 1212 from Emperor Frederick II. This gave the Bohemian king the right of investiture of bishops. Otakar I was also successful in settling feudal disputes and the kingdom flourished. Under his son, Václav I (1230-1253), new towns were established, German immigrants settled in the area and trade prospered. Mining was also developed, especially silver in Jihlava and Kutná Hora. The Czech coin, the groš, became one of the most valuable and widely used currencies in Central Europe.

Expansion was sought under King Přemysl Otakar II (1253-1278) who attempted to conquer part of Austria but was defeated and killed in battle in 1278. His son Wenceslas (Václav) II, restored Bohemia's power and

A 19th century engraving of Český Šternberk Castle.

after a successful campaign in Poland received the Polish crown. On his death in 1305, his son Wenceslas III succeeded him. His assassination a year later signalled the end of the House of Přemyslids.

The crown was contested for the next five years and in 1310 it was offered to King John of Luxembourg (1310-1346). He founded the Bohemian branch of the Luxembourg house which ruled Bohemia for a century.

His son, Charles, was a powerful ruler, holding the post of Higher Administrator of Moravia from 1333. He was crowned King Charles I of Bohemia in 1346 and Charles IV, Holy Roman Emperor in 1355. He extended the lands ruled by the Czech crown by adding Upper and Lower Lusatia, Silesia and Brandeburg. During his reign Prague became the capital of the Holy Roman Empire. Charles founded the first university in Central Europe (1348), upgraded Prague bishopric to an archbishopric (1344) and gave privileges to the church and wealthy patricians. But under his rule, and that of his son Wenceslas IV (1378-1419), social discontent, especially against the power of the church, intensified.

An increasing number of Czechs espoused the Reformation and its leader John Huss (Jan Hus). Their campaign to reform the church became the dominant factor in the history of Bohemia for several decades. When Huss was burnt at the stake as a heretic on July 6, 1415 civil war broke out. The result was a conflict which lasted for two decades.

Attempts by Wenceslas' brother, Sigismund, to break the Hussites' resistance were initially unsuccessful. But Sigismund was able to restore his authority over the country after the defeat of the Hussite forces at Lipany in 1434. He was proclaimed king in 1436, but died the following year.

After their defeat, Hussite lords formed a political movement to promote national interests. A number of moderate Catholics joined them to form a national movement. In 1444 George of Poděbrady was named leader of the movement, which by now represented a strong majority of the population. He was appointed Governor of Bohemia in 1451. When Ladislav, grandson of Sigismund was crowned king in 1453, George became his advisor and a valuable ally and Ladislav, a Catholic, now had the backing of the national movement. On Ladislav's death, the estates of Bohemia elected George of Poděbrady king. He was crowned on March 2, 1458. The Hussite king became known for his proposal to establish an association of European rulers in order to preserve peace. George favoured an elected monarchy and chose not to nominate his son as his successor to the throne.

On his death Vladislav of the Polish Lithuanian dynasty (1471-1516) was elected King of Bohemia. During his reign the nobility acquired unprecedented power both at the expense of the king and the middle classes. In 1490 Vladislav was also elected King of Hungary. He was succeeded by his son Louis II who waged war unsuccessfully against the Turks, leading to the defeat at Mohacs and his own death in 1526.

Archduke Ferdinand I of the Habsburg dynasty claimed the throne and his election as King of Bohemia established a multinational monarchy which included Austria and Hungary. The Habsburgs were to rule Bohemia until 1918. Ferdinand worked hard to restore the power of the monarchy by restricting the rights of the towns and the nobility.

Religion was to prove the major seed of contention. Much of the population had espoused Protestantism, but Ferdinand, a firm Catholic, took the opportunity of the defeat of the German Protestants in Mühlberg to clamp down on the towns and boost the Catholic church.

Despite Habsburg rule, Bohemia prospered and

reached its peak under Rudolph II (1576-1612) when Rudolph moved the imperial seat from Vienna to Prague. Rudolph attempted to resolve religious strife by issuing a decree granting freedom of religion. But this decree was not honoured by Ferdinand II. The protests that followed led to a full-scale revolt.

The Czechs raised an army and attacked the Habsburgs, but were defeated by Catholic forces at the Battle of Bílá Hora (White Mountain) in 1620. The leaders of the revolt were executed and thousands of Czech families went into exile. The Czech lands were divested of their privileges and were added to the Habsburg monarchy. A new Catholic nobility was established, and Bohemia became the battleground of the Thirty Year's War (1618-1648).

Bohemia, exhausted by the wars and depopulation, fell into decline. The rural class was now the main representative of the nation. For almost two centuries under various Habsburg kings, the Czechs survived largely as a rural people. Under Maria Theresa (1740-1780) their living conditions improved and continued to do so under her son, Joseph II, (1780-1790) who passed the Edict of Toleration granting freedom of religion. At the same time he passed a decree restoring personal liberty to the peasants which later led to the abolition of serfdom.

A national awakening began in the 18th century as a result of these reforms and economic development. The Czechs began moving into the towns and slowly began to regain their cultural identity. The Czech language and culture were revived in the form of theatre and literature while the sciences thrived.

In 1848, as the winds of change swept through Europe, the Czechs made political demands including the federalisation of the Habsburg monarchy into ethnic units and unity with the Slovaks. Their subsequent revolt was suppressed and the only gain was the abolition of serfdom on September 7, 1848.

The Czechs' national demands were ignored again in 1867 with the establishment of the Austro-Hungarian Empire and, despite economic progress, political reform was slow and piecemeal.

A group of Slovaks, 19th century engraving.

THE SLOVAKS

In the ninth century, Slavs living in today's Slovakia created the Nitra Principality, which was added to the Great Moravian Empire under Prince Pribina. It was at this time that Christianity was introduced by the Greek bishops Cyril and Methodius. In the 10th century the Slavs faced the threat of the Magyars who began to build their own state. After the 1018 peace treaty between Stephen and Boleslav the Brave, the Magyars began to expand to the north. By 1030 the Magyar House of Arpad ruled western Slovakia. By the 12th century Slovakia had been completely incorporated into Hungary.

In 1222, under King Andrew II, the nobility acquired excessive privileges. This hampered resistance against the invading Tatars who plundered a great deal of the country in 1241. In the second half of the 13th century German colonists were encouraged to settle in the area.

When the House of Arpad died out in 1301, a period of confusion followed. Slovakia was ruled by oligarchs until the House of Anjou seized power in 1308. Under the Anjous, the monarchy flourished and towns in Slovakia developed. The Anjous were followed by King Sigismund of Luxembourg who fought against the Turks and the Hussites. Slovakia was ransacked by Hussites who took over many towns including Trnava, Skalice, Trenčín and Kežmarok in their battle against Sigismund.

Under Matthias Corvinus (1458-1490) the king's power was strengthened and Moravia was added to the Hungarian state. The university of Bratislava was also

Stained glass window from St. Vitus Cathedral, Prague.

Hungary. The defeat of the Turks at Vienna in 1683, the taking of Buda and the gradual expulsion of the Turks led to the strengthening of the Habsburgs.

It proved more difficult for the nationalist movement to develop in Slovakia than in the Czech Lands. The first signs of nationalism were efforts by Anton Bernolák to develop a Slovak literary language. He failed but in 1844 Ljudovit Štúr and his generation succeeded. The same activists also called for the abolition of feudalism.

But the Slovak national movement was weakened during the 1848-1849 revolution when neither the Hungarian revolutionaries, who tore apart from Austria in 1849, nor the conservatives gave heed to their demands. Although their uprising was crushed by the Magyars, their subordinate dependence on Hungary was abolished.

Slovak nationalism came to the fore again with the Martin Memorandum of the Slovak nation in 1861 and the Matice Slovenská in 1863. Hopes that the nationalist movement would grow were thwarted when the December 1867 constitution of the Austro-Hungarian Empire gave the Hungarians increased power. In 1868 Slovak national identity was further threatened by a law incorporating all ethnic groups into one political nation.

THE TWENTIETH CENTURY

founded under Matthias, but the state was weakened after his death. Power fell into the hands of magnates of the powerful House of Zapoli. The defeat to the Turks at Mohacs under Louis II led to the effective partition of Hungary. Slovakia, Croatia and Western Hungary came under the Habsburgs.

Slovakia was the battleground in the numerous campaigns fought against the Turks in the 16th and 17th centuries. The situation was further complicated by numerous rebellions of the non-Catholic nobility of

At the outbreak of World War I, the Czechs took the opportunity to press for complete independence from the Habsburg Empire through a combination of diplomacy abroad and passive resistance at home. Meanwhile, Slovak opposition to the Austrians and Hungarians was manifested by rebellions and army revolts. Czech diplomatic initiatives were undertaken and Czech soldiers fought with the allies.

On November 14, 1915 a manifesto was issued supporting the Entente powers and Czech and Slovak independence. In January 1916 the National Czech Council was formed with Tomáš Garrigue Masaryk as president. On January 6, 1918 the Epiphany Convention in Prague attended by all Czech members of the Reichsrat and diets of Bohemia, Moravia and Silesia, concluded with a demand for a sovereign state. In May of the same year Masaryk attended a meeting in Pittsburgh, USA, of American Czechs and Slovaks and signed a statement in support of the unity of the two peoples. At the same time, the Slovak national party agreed to join the Czech nation.

On October 14, the Entente states were notified of the establishment of an interim Czech government in Prague. On October 28, the National Committee in Prague proclaimed the independence of Czech territories and two days later in Slovakia the Slovak National Council pronounced itself in favour of unity with the Czechs. The independent republic was quickly recognised by the allies.

The new state, a multi-party democracy based on the French and American models, guaranteed universal suffrage, human rights and equal rights to all its nationalities. Its first president was Tomáš Masaryk who retired from power in 1935. He was succeeded by his foreign minister Edvard Beneš.

Czechoslovakia, the first democratic country in Central Europe, was ruled by a stable government made up of a five-party coalition known as the Petka. But it faced the problem of smoothing out differences with its sizeable minority groups, the Sudeten Germans, Hungarians, Poles and Ruthenes, and protecting its territorial integrity. In order to safeguard its borders, Czechoslovakia entered into various agreements with neighbouring countries including the Little Entente with Yugoslavia and Romania in 1921, an alliance with France in 1925 and an alliance with the Soviet Union in 1935. The country initially flourished, but as the international economic crisis began to take its toll, dissatisfaction grew among the minorities.

The Sudeten Germans were especially hit by the depression and this fanned the flames of growing nationalism. In the general elections of May 1935 the Sudeten German party, a nationalist movement led by Konrád Henlein, won 66 per cent of the German vote.

Stained glass window from St. Vitus Cathedral, Prague.

Heavily subsidised by Nazi Germany, the party pressed for political concessions to the German minority. Czechoslovakia soon found that without help from Europe it was unable to stand up to the Nazis.

After the Anschluss between Germany and Austria in 1938, Hitler quickly began to make demands on Czechoslovakia. He threatened war unless the Sudetenland was ceded, and Britain, France and Italy succumbed. Czechoslovakia was not even present at the Munich conference of September 30, 1938 which

9

sealed its fate. France and Britain agreed to Hitler's demands, and realising Czechoslovakia could not fend off Hitler on its own, Beneš capitulated.

German troops entered the Sudetenland on October 1, 1938. Soon after Poland took control of the Teschen district in northern Moravia and Hungary took over much of southern Slovakia. Overall Czechoslovakia lost 30 per cent of its territory, one third of its population, including 1.3 million Czechs and Slovaks, and 40 per cent of its industrial capacity and was left strategically defenceless.

Beneš resigned on October 5, 1938, and went into exile while the Nazi intrigues continued, culminating in total Nazi subjugation within a few months. On March 14, 1939 a Slovak state was declared loyal to the Nazis. The following day the remainder of the country was occupied by the Nazis who proclaimed a protectorate of Bohemia-Moravia.

During the War, Czechoslovakia's industrial capacity was exploited to the full by the Nazis. The intelligentsia was suppressed and Jews were persecuted. But the Czechs and Slovaks never accepted Nazi domination. Anti-Nazi demonstrations in Prague in October and November 1939 led to the arrest of hundreds of students. Thousands fought against the Nazis abroad, while the greatest anti-Nazi demonstration was the Slovak National Rising in 1944 which engaged Nazi troops for two whole months. The May rising in Bohemia in 1945 speeded up the end of the war. Prague was freed by the Red Army on May 9, 1945 and western Bohemia was liberated by the American army.

Meanwhile, Beneš had set up a Czechoslovak government in exile and persuaded the allies to repudiate the Munich agreements. In March 1945 members of the London-based government travelled to Moscow where they agreed with the Czechoslovak Communist Party to form a National Front government. The new government announced its programme on April 5, 1945 at Košice in eastern Slovakia behind Red Army lines. It included free elections, nationalisation and land reforms. The government was installed in Prague on May 10, 1945 with Beneš as president.

At the instigation of the communists, the government banned all parties outside the coalition, reserved key ministries for the communists, nationalised banking, insurance and key industries and redistributed the land of the collaborators.

In June 1945 Ruthenia was signed over to the Soviet Union. In the May 1946 election the Communist Party surfaced as the largest party with almost 38 per cent of the vote. It joined forces with the Social Democrats in the National Assembly to secure a left wing majority of 151 of the 300 seats, pitted against the National Socialist Party, the People's Party and the Slovak Democratic Party. Beneš was re-elected president but the premiership of the new National Front coalition government went to Communist leader Klement Gottwald. Most ministerial positions also went to the Communists. But Jan Masaryk, son of the country's first president remained Foreign Minister.

But there was soon trouble in the coalition government as relations between the parties became increasingly strained. The non-communists were opposed to the nationalisation of land, and the reorganisation of the police. By January 1948 the rift was so great that the government was almost paralysed. In February the non-communist ministers resigned and Gottwald refused to re-admit the ministers into a new government. Against a background of communist-instigated work councils, trade unions and armed militias patrolling the streets, Gottwald warned Beneš that there would be civil war unless he accepted the appointment of a new cabinet. Beneš backed down and in the new government control rested with the communists.

The communists had taken power "legally" in what was later described as a bloodless coup. Jan Masaryk remained Foreign Minister but within days, on March 10 he was found dead on the pavement under the window of his official residence.

On May 9, the National Assembly, rid of opposition, approved a new Soviet-style constitution, but Beneš refused to sign it. In the new elections held on May 30, the electorate was presented with a single list of candidates. Beneš resigned on June 7 and was succeeded by Gottwald. Czechoslovakia became a one-party state with a centrally planned economy. Agriculture was collectivised on the Soviet model in 1949, remaining private businesses were nationalised while the five year plan of 1951 laid emphasis on the development of heavy industry.

The purges, in the wake of the February coup intensified in the Stalinist years that followed. Leading communists, including Gustav Husák, future president, were imprisoned in 1950. Others, including Vladimir Clementis, Czechoslovakia's representative to the United Nations, and Rudolf Slánský, the Communist Party general secretary, were executed while the Catholic church was suppressed.

Gottwald died in 1953, but under Antonín Novotný, party leader and later president, Czechoslovakia remained almost untouched by the liberalisation process while the relative economic prosperity served as a stabilising factor. In 1960 the country's new constitution renamed the country Czechoslovak Socialist Republic and confirmed the Communist Party's leading role in society.

But in the 1960s the economic situation deteriorated and with it came the decision to liberalise. Former communists were rehabilitated and the new Prime Minister, Jozef Lenárt, embarked on a new economic course. Dissent became increasingly vocal, especially through the Czechoslovak Writers' Congress, and the reformists gradually gained the upper hand. Novotný was suddenly replaced as party chief in January 1968, ushering in the Prague Spring. The new party secretary Alexander Dubček pledged to build "Socialism with a Human Face". He unveiled a programme aimed at democratising the Communist Party, liberalising restrictions of the press and introducing greater popular participation.

In March Novotný was replaced as president by General Ludvig Svoboda. In the ensuing liberalisation, Czechoslovaks were free to travel to the west and censorship was practically abolished as Dubček began trying to reform the constitution.

The situation in Czechoslovakia worried its East Bloc allies. On August 21, troops from the Soviet Union, Poland, Hungary, East Germany and Bulgaria invaded Czechoslovakia and Dubček and the party leadership were arrested and taken to Moscow. There was passive resistance and demonstrations in the streets and opposition by the Communist Party which on August 22 voted overwhelmingly in favour of Dubček.

Dubček was obliged to accept a treaty normalising the presence of Soviet troops in Czechoslovakia or face force. The Prague Spring had ended. In April 1969 Dubček was replaced as party secretary by Dr. Gustav Husák. In September he was expelled from the party presidium and in June 1970 expelled from the party altogether. The purges went deep into the Communist Party, trade unions and universities and thousands chose to emigrate.

Czechoslovak sentiment regarding the suppression of the Prague Spring was graphically portrayed by the student Jan Pallach who set himself on fire in January 1969 in protest.

Meanwhile, resistance continued. On August 21, 1969 first anniversary of the invasion, the "Ten Points Manifesto" was published. Reformists who set up the underground Socialist Movement of Czechoslovak Citizens were suppressed in early 1971. But the underground continued through the press and pop music. The opposition resurfaced in 1977 with the Charter 77 group. The Charter, signed by 240 intellectuals, was formed to appeal for the implementation of human rights, including freedom of expression and religion.

Charter 77 caught the imagination of the west and united former communists and non-communists in a campaign for human rights. Many Charter 77 signatories were persecuted, but the pressure on the Communist regime continued, encouraged by the reformist policies of Soviet leader Michail Gorbachev.

Pressure gained momentum as the winds of change swept through Eastern Europe. At the beginning of 1989 demonstrations were held to mark the death of Jan Pallach. Havel and 13 other dissidents were arrested. On June 29, a document called Several Sentences was published, demanding dialogue with the authorities as

Karlsbrücke, Prague.

A 19th century engraving of Charles Bridge.

the only way to bring Czechoslovakia out of the impasse.

Things came to a head in November, as a student demonstration took on the momentum of a peaceful people's uprising, known as the Velvet Revolution. On November 17 thousands of students staged a demonstration to mark the death in 1939 of student Jan Opletal, killed in an anti-Nazi demonstration. The demonstration was put down by force. Students immediately went on strike, led by the Damu drama school. They were joined by musicians, actors and other theatre workers as thousands of demonstrators, mostly young people, packed out Wenceslas Square in a continuing campaign for democratisation. One highlight was November 24 when Dubček came back from obscurity to join Havel in addressing the crowds. The demonstrators were supported by the workers who on November 27 went on a brief general strike.

On November 19 more than a dozen opposition groups met in Prague to form an opposition coalition, the Civic Forum. The following day a sister organisation, Public Against Violence, was founded in Slovakia. Both were headed by Charter 77 activists.

The premier, Ladislav Adamec, sought negotiations with the Civic Forum. But events were also unfolding in the National Assembly. On November 29 it voted to end the Communist Party's monopoly of power. When it became known that Adamec's new cabinet included several communists it prompted further demonstrations. He resigned on December 7 and Civic Forum put forward its own list to outgoing president Husák.

A government of National Unity was formed and two weeks later Civic Forum leader Václav Havel was elected president on December 29. The Velvet Revolution, with Havel at its head, succeeded in achieving multi-party democracy. New parties surfaced and in the elections of June 8, 1990 there was a 96.7 per cent turnout. Civic Forum and its Slovak branch won a clear majority in both federal chambers. A coalition government was formed, Havel was re-elected president and work began on a new constitution. In 1991 Czechoslovakia became the second East European country to join the Council of Europe.

[Latin text of the Nuremberg Chronicle, in two columns, describing Prague (Praga caput regni bohemie ciuitas primaria...). Text set in gothic type with numerous contractions.]

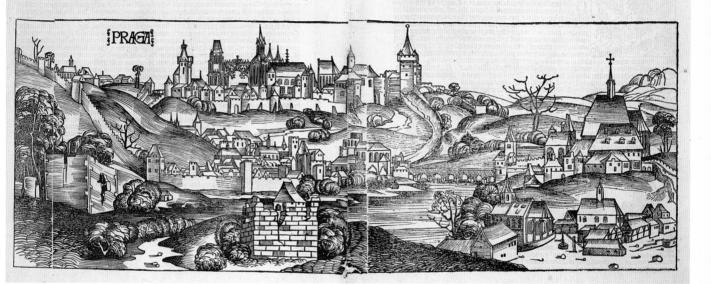

View of Prague engraved in the 15th century.

PRAGUE - INTRODUCTION

Prague (Praha), the capital of the Czech and Slovak Federal Republic and the Czech republic covers an area of 497 square kms and has a population of 1.2 million. Situated in the heart of Europe, Prague is built on both banks of the river Vltava and on the surrounding forested hills, the most notable of which are Hradčany, Vyšehrad and Petřín. Most of the city is built 200 m above sea level. The highest point (383 m) is Bílá Hora (White Mountain).

The skyline of the city is dominated by Prague Castle and graced by dozens of spires which account for Prague's description as the "city of one hundred spires". Another landmark is Charles Bridge, the oldest and best known of the 14 road and railway bridges which span the Vltava.

One of the best preserved medieval cities of Europe, Prague retains all the glory and elegance befitting its rich historical past. Having survived the onslaught of time and escaped the destruction of World War II, Prague benefitted from a concerted conservation campaign.

Indicative of this is the city's system of numbering historical buildings. Most have two numbers on blue and red plaques. The blue plaque indicates the number of the street and the red plaque the order in which the building was registered with the municipality -- the smaller the number the older the building.

General view of the bridges of Prague from Letná Hill.

Prague's architectural treasures, ranging from exquisitely ornamented palaces to imposing churches, span 1,000 years. They combine with rich art collections and important musical events to justify its renown as one of the cultural capitals of the world.

Prague is today divided into 10 districts. But it is its five historic towns that are of most interest: Hradčany, Malá Strana (Lesser Quarter), Staré Město (Old Town), Josefov (the former Jewish quarter) and Nové Město (New Town). Prague also offers possibilities for excursions to Bohemia's historic towns and castles.

PRAGUE - HISTORICAL SURVEY

Legend has it that Prague was founded at the bequest of Libuše, (Libussa) wife of Přemysl, who foretold a brilliant future for the city. Acting on her wishes Přemysl and his followers discovered the site described by Libussa and built Prague.

In fact, the development of Prague is inextricably linked with Prague Castle on Hradčany.

The Castle was founded by Prince Bořivoj and his wife Ludmilla in the last quarter of the ninth century on the hills overlooking the river Vltava. Bořivoj moved his seat here from Levý Hradec.

In the first half of the 10th century Chrasten Castle (Vyšehrad) was founded on the opposite bank. Both castles afforded protection to the trading settlements established on the banks of the river at the crossroads of the trade routes. By the 10th century the city was already an important trading centre. The House of Přemyslid used Prague in order to unify all Bohemia and spread Christianity. Bořivoj and Ludmilla, were converted to Christianity by the Greek Bishop Methodius while their grandson Wenceslas became the patron saint of Bohemia.

The House of Přemyslid flourished, becoming so important that it was given the title of King of Bohemia by the Holy Roman Emperor. The first king to bear this title was Prince Vratislav II in 1085.

Prague's first bishopric was established in 973 and the construction of many stone churches such as the Church of the Virgin Mary, St. Vitus and St. George soon followed.

At first settlement was restricted to the left bank of the river under the Castle. But from the 11th century on communities began to develop on the right bank and by the 13th century covered 70 hectares and later developed into the Staré Město or Old Town.

From the 12th century on, Prague Castle and Vyšehrad were reconstructed in the Romanesque style. Other important buildings, among them Strahov monastery, the Bishop's Court, and several churches and houses in the Malá Strana (Lesser Town), were also built in this style. Judith Bridge was constructed in 1170.

Under Wenceslas II (1230-1253) the city was organised with laws and an army. Fortifications were built around the city. Wenceslas' son, Přemysl Otakar II (1253-1278) fortified the Malá Strana, connected it with the Hradčany, and invited German colonists to settle there.

The centres of both towns (Malá Strana and Staré Město) were the new market place, now known as the Old Town Square where the Royal Custom House stood, and Malá Strana Square. New churches, including St. Anežka's, (St. Agnes) were built and a web of streets developed in Staré Město as Gothic influences became evident in the architecture.

Prague continued to grow under the Luxembourg dynasty (1310-1437). The expansion of the population obliged Charles IV (1346-1378) to found the Nové Město (New Town) of Prague in 1348 in an area of 360 hectares. The town was fortified, horse, cattle and hay markets established while, in Hradčany, the Castle, St. Vitus Cathedral and St. George's Monastery were redecorated. Charles made Prague the capital of the Holy Roman Empire. He promoted the bishopric into an archbishopric in 1344, founded Charles University in 1348, and built Charles Bridge to replace Judith Bridge. Charles also enlarged and redecorated Vyšehrad.

After his death, under his son Wenceslas IV, national, social and religious differences came to the fore. Prague began to decline and the situation was aggravated when Wenceslas lost his title as Holy Roman Emperor in 1400.

Less fortunate Czechs angry at the rich, mostly foreign aristocracy and the clergy, paid heed to the preachers of the Reformation. Chief among them was Jan Hus (John Huss), whose inflammatory ideas incensed the church and many Czech nobles. He was sentenced to burn at the stake as a heretic in 1415 and

View of Hradčany from Charles Bridge.

many of his supporters were arrested. His execution laid the seeds of what was to develop into a crucial period in Czech history. On July 30th, 1419, an angry mob stormed the New Town Hall, demanding the release of the Hussites and threw the German councillors out of the window in the first of Prague's famous defenestrations. Their actions sparked off the Hussite Wars.

After the death of Wenceslas IV in 1419 the people of Prague continued in their protest. They attacked churches and monasteries, and set fire to the Malá Strana. Pope Martin V sent crusaders to Prague in 1420 and again in 1421 to subdue the heretics, but the Hussites won at the Battle of Vítkov in 1420 and in 1421 forced Prague Castle to capitulate and expelled the German aristocracy.

A winter view of Prague from Petřín Hill.

Under the Hussites Prague lost much of its commerce and the economy stagnated. After a period of instability George of Poděbrady, a Hussite, took power in Prague in 1448 and ten years later was crowned King of Bohemia. But the Pope excommunicated George and encouraged the Roman Catholics to rise against him. He was finally defeated in 1471.

The throne went to Vladislav II of the Polish Lithuanian family (1471-1516) who tried to restore Catholicism. This led to further riots by the Hussites and the second defenestration (1483). Vladislav transferred his seat from Králův Dvůr (King's Court) in the Old Town to Prague Castle, which was rebuilt at his command in the late Gothic style.

In 1518, during the reign of Vladislav's son Louis, the Old and New Towns were united. After Louis' death in 1526, the throne was claimed by his brother-in-law Ferdinand I who dissolved the unity of Prague in 1528 and removed the Hussite Jan Pašek of Vrat as administrator of the two towns. The city lost its prerogatives and much of its property and was subordinated to the Habsburgs.

Prague reached the height of its glory under Emperor Rudolf II (1583-1612) who moved the imperial capital from Vienna to Prague. The city flourished and became a major artistic and scientific centre in Europe. Religious differences, however, persisted and riots became practically an everyday event. The Protestants capitalised on Rudolf's differences with his brother Matthias, and obliged Rudolf to grant religious freedom in 1609. Two years later Rudolf was forced to abdicate in favour of Matthias.

The conflicts, however, did not stop. The Protestants revolted and on May 23, 1618 two Catholic governors and their secretary were defenestrated. This led to an uprising headed by a small number of nobles. Within two and half years the Habsburgs were removed from the throne and the Czechs elected Frederick V, a Protestant, Elector of the Palatinate, King of Bohemia. But Catholic Europe regrouped and hit back defeating the Bohemians at the Battle of Bílá Hora (White Mountain) in 1620. Prague fell to the armies of the Catholic League and King Frederick was forced to flee.

The town was plundered, property was confiscated, non-Catholics forced to emigrate and 27 citizens of Prague, including 10 nobles and knights, were executed in the Old Town Square. By 1624 Catholicism was the only religion permitted in Bohemia.

The years 1618-1648 were characterised by the ravaging Thirty Year's War during which the economy stagnated and Prague was reduced to a provincial town. The war hit Prague twice: first in 1631-1632 when it was occupied by Saxon troops and again in 1648-1649 when Malá Strana and Prague Castle were occupied by Swedish troops.

As a result of the war few architectural projects were commissioned. However, the magnificent palace of Albrecht von Wallenstein in the Malá Strana was built in this period. In the second half of the 17th century Baroque influences gradually overshadowed the Gothic style. Important monuments redecorated in the Baroque style include the Palace of Černín in Hradčany, Loreta Chapel, Strahov Monastery, and the Church of St. Nicholas in Malá Strana.

At the start of Maria Theresa's reign (1740-1780) Prague was conquered by Bavarian, Saxon and French troops. In 1744 Prussian troops encircled Prague for three weeks and a number of buildings were destroyed during the siege.

Maria Theresa initiated a series of reforms which

A winter view of Malá Strana and Hradčany.

allowed the population to grow and the economy to flourish. The influence of the church was reduced and several public service buildings were constructed. In 1753 Prague Castle was again renovated. In 1773 the Jesuit order was dissolved and its wealth was taken over by the government of Bohemia. Further reforms were undertaken by her son, Joseph II (1780-90). He abolished forced labour prompting many peasants to leave their villages and come to Prague. He also enacted the Edict of Toleration in 1781 guaranteeing equal rights to Catholics and Protestants and thus ending the religious wars.

In 1784 the four towns of Prague were united and their town councils merged into one municipality. The nobles, however, insisted on their privileges and resisted efforts to centralise power. A national movement was created in an attempt to save the Czech language.

Several nationalist organisations were established, among them the Royal Czech Association of Doctrines (1784), the Patriotic Economic Association (1769), the Association of the Patriotic Friends of Fine Arts (1796), the Conservatory of Music (1811) and the Association of the Patriotic Museum (1818) helping to establish Prague as a major cultural centre.

Prague's economy stagnated in the wake of the Napoleonic wars, but the impact of the industrial revolution fuelled its development. The population in the outskirts grew as the city acquired a sewage system, gas lighting and better transport, including a railway connection with Olomouc and Vienna.

During this time the nationalist movement was strengthened, and moving beyond efforts to preserve language and culture, made political demands. The National Museum Foundation associated with famous writers, thinkers and journalists, served as the cradle for burgeoning nationalism.

The movement began presenting petitions to the Vienna government asking for democratic reform and autonomy. In 1848 a Conference of Slavs meeting in Prague to discuss reforms was dispersed by force, as Prague students and workers joined the movement against the Vienna government. The latter responded by imposing martial law, which lasted four years, and jailing and executing the ringleaders.

The reign of King Franz Joseph (1848-1916) was also authoritarian, but the economy prospered and Prague expanded. Other districts were incorporated into the city of Prague including Josefov (1850), Vyšehrad (1883), Holešovice (1884) and Libeň (1901). In 1871 the town walls were pulled down and by 1883 the construction of the National Theatre was completed. In 1890 the buildings of the National Museum were renovated.

With the outbreak of World War I, however, development came to a complete standstill. The defeat of the Austro-Hungarian Empire led to the establishment of the independent Republic of Czechoslovakia with Prague as the capital and Prague Castle as the seat of the government. In 1922 the Patent of Larger Towns was adopted and Prague grew to include 32 communities. Development was again interrupted by World War II and the Nazi occupation.

After the War Prague continued to develop. In 1968 it captured the world's headlines with the Prague Spring, which was put down within a few months following the invasion of Warsaw Pact forces. Some twenty years later the people of Prague once more took to the streets paving the way for the Velvet Revolution which peacefully overthrew the one-party system and restored multi-party democracy to this Central European nation.

A 19th century engraving of Prague.

HRADČANY AND PRAGUE CASTLE

Prague Castle was founded in the last quarter of the ninth century by legendary Prince Bořivoj as a Slav castle with towers and moats. Bořivoj was converted to Christianity by Bishop Methodius.

During the 10th century a number of churches were built, including St. George and St. Vitus. The Prince's Palace on the southern side of the Castle as well as the first Benedictine Convent beside the Church of St. George and the Bishop's Palace were also built in the 10th century. The archaeological discoveries (jewellery found in tombs) prove the strong cultural influence of Great Moravia even after its decline in the early 10th century.

The Castle was named after one of the most influential men of the House of Přemyslid, Prince Wenceslas who died in 929. In 1004 the Castle was conquered by troops of Henry II, the Holy Roman Emperor and the Polish-Czech Garrison was dispersed. The Castle was destroyed by Henry III (1041) and new fortifications were built by Prince Břetislav I (1037-1055) and his sons Spytihněv II (1055-1061) and Vratislav II (1061-1092) who became the Czech king in 1085.

Romanesque elements were added as from 1135 during the reigns of Soběslav I (1125-1140) and Vladislav II (1140-1173). Fortifications were constructed in the Roman style to encircle the Castle while the Prince's Palace, the Church of All Saints, the Church of St. George and the Bishop's Palace were rebuilt.

The Castle was damaged by fire during the siege of Conrad of Znojmo in 1142. During the reign of Přemysl Otakar II (1253-1278) nicknamed the Iron and Golden King new moats with walls were constructed and the Royal Palace was rebuilt. The Castle experienced its golden age under King Charles IV (1346-1378) who rebuilt the Royal Palace, St. Vitus Cathedral, the Church of All Saints and the Church of St. George in the late

View of Charles Bridge and Hradčany from Staré Město.

Gothic style. Charles IV also enriched the treasury of St. Vitus and extended the library. The most significant architects were Matthias of Arras and Peter Parléř.

Charles' son Wenceslas IV (1378-1419) moved the royal seat from the Castle to the Staré Město. Prague citizens seized control of the Castle in 1421 and held it until 1434. It did not serve a residential purpose until the reign of Vladislav II (1471-1516) who fortified it further by adding the towers of Mihulka, Bílá and Daliborka. It was during this period that Vladislav Hall, (a ceremonial hall that still retains its importance) and Vladislav's bedroom were completed and took his name. The chancellery and the Louis (Ludvík) Wing with the Green Room were also completed in this period.

After the death of Louis the Habsburg Ferdinand I was elected Czech king. Ferdinand founded the Royal Garden, connected to the Castle by the Powder Bridge (1534). After a fire on June 2, 1541, St. Vitus Cathedral, the Royal Palace, the Palaces of Rožmberk, Pernštein and other buildings were reconstructed in the Renaissance style. Ferdinand's successors, Maximilian II (1564-1576) and Rudolf II (1576-1611) enlarged the Royal Garden and added the Lví Dvůr (Lion's Court) and the Large and Small Ballrooms (Velká a Malá Míčovna)

Rudolf converted the Castle into an arts and scientific centre. He gathered numerous collections of paintings, statues and other artistic objects and patronised such artists and scientists as Hans van Aachen, Bartolomej Spranger, Josef Heinz, Tycho de Brahe and Jan Kepler. In 1614 the Habsburgs moved the royal seat to Vienna and the Castle lost its residential function.

On May 23, 1618 the governors Vilém Slavata and Jaroslav Bořita of Martinic were thrown out of the window from the Louis Wing in one of Prague's famous defenestrations prompting an uprising and later the Thirty Year's War. When the Hussites were crushed at the Battle of Bílá Hora (White Mountain) in 1620 the Castle became just another of the Habsburgs' seats and was used mainly for coronations.

During the Thirty Year's War the Castle was

The western entrance to Prague Castle.

View of Prague Castle from Hradčany Square.

occupied by the Saxons (1631-32) and by the Swedes (1648-49). Much damage was inflicted and Rudolf's collection was carted off to Sweden. In the second half of the 17th century St. George's Monastery was enlarged, Lobkowicz Palace reconstructed and the Castle's Gallery was enriched. In the first half of the 18th century the interiors of many churches and palaces were redecorated.

The Castle was conquered in 1741 by Bavarians, Saxons and their French allies. In 1744 it was seriously damaged by the Prussians and it was again damaged during the Seven Year's War in 1757.

The Castle took its current appearance during the reign of Empress Maria Theresa (1740-1780) based on the late Baroque designs of architect N. Pacassi. Joseph II (1780-1790) converted the Castle into artillery barracks, abolished St. George's Monastery and auctioned off all the Castle's collections.

Its significance declined in the 19th century the only enlivenment being the coronations and the all too rare visits of the Habsburgs. The planned coronation of Franz Joseph (1848-1916) as Czech king did not take place and therefore the decorations envisaged for the

The ceremonial changing of the guard in the First Courtyard.

The Matthias Gate.

occasion were carried out only on the Spanish Hall and Rudolph's Gallery. The only major project was the completion of St. Vitus Cathedral in 1873-1929 by architects J. Mocker and K. Hilbert.

With the establishment of the independent Republic of Czechoslovakia in 1918 the Castle became the seat of the president and was modernised and decorated according to the plans of architect J. Plečnik. The Palace was renovated and researched by K. Fiala. Systematic excavations commenced in 1925 still continue. Important discoveries include the foundations of the original rotunda and basilica of St. Vitus, the Bishop's Chapel and Castle fortifications. Renovation stopped during World War II. Excavations after the War revealed the Church of the Virgin Mary discovered in 1950, the interiors of St. George (1958-1963) and the ninth and 10th century children's and women's cemeteries.

After the end of the War, the Míčovna (Ball Hall) burnt down during the War, was reconstructed. The sgraffiti were restored and the Letohrádek (Belvedere) and Jízdárna (Riding Room) were converted into Exhibitions Halls and the interiors of the Middle, Western and Southern wings were modernised. In 1975 the Jiřský Klášter (St. George's Monastery) was converted into the Bohemian Art Gallery. Since 1987 Lobkowicz Palace has housed historical exhibits of the National Museum. The ground floor of the northern wing was converted into an art gallery in 1965 and since 1961 some treasures from St. Vitus Cathedral have been exhibited in the Chapel of the Holy Cross. The Powder Tower (Mihulka) was opened to the public in 1982.

One of the two statues of giants guarding the western entrance to the Castle.

View of the Northern Gate and St. Vitus Cathedral .

The Mihulka Tower and St. Vitus Cathedral.

PRAGUE CASTLE - ITINERARY

Prague Castle, which occupies the eastern part of Hradčany has three entrances, the main gate at Hradčany Square to the west, the Powder Bridge to the north and up the old Castle steps to the east.

From Hradčany Square the main gate with its statues of giants (copies of the originals created by F.L. Platzer in 1901-02) and the lattice fence leads to the First Courtyard where the ceremonial changing of the guard takes place. Matthias Gate, built in the early Baroque style in 1614, leads to the Second Courtyard. The entry to the Spanish Hall is below the arch of the Gate on the left. On the right a ceremonial staircase leads to the state rooms.

The Second Courtyard is enclosed by the Theresian style buildings of the Castle wings. Beside the southern wing is the Holy Cross Chapel, which houses treasures from St. Vitus Cathedral. On the ground floor of the northern and western wings is the Picture Gallery of Prague Castle. The Kohl fountain, dating back to 1686, is situated in the middle of the courtyard. A gateway leads to the Third Courtyard which occupies the central area of the Castle.

The Third Courtyard is paved with reinforced concrete tiles which cover inaccessible archaeological deposits. St. Vitus Cathedral dominates the courtyard. Next to the Cathedral is the building of the old Provost (originally a bishop's house). Its recent Baroque appearance dates to 1701. A Mrákotín granite monolith was erected next to it (1928). Close by is the Gothic-Renaissance style equestrian statue of St. George renovated many times through the years. Its pedestal and basin were designed by J. Plečnik in 1928. The Royal Palace is located to the south-west of St. Vitus.

The Third Courtyard leads to St. George's Square and St. George's Basilica. The former convent next to the Basilica is now the Bohemian Art Gallery.

Jiřská Street leads from the square towards the eastern end of the Castle. The Palace of the Rožmberk family was built in 1545 on the site of several Renaissance houses. It later became an Institute of Gentlewomen, a home for the female members of impoverished aristocratic families.

On the eastern end of the street is Lobkowicz Palace. Its present appearance dates to 1651. In 1973 the Palace was reconstructed and is now used as a historical exposition of the National Museum.

Nearby, the Eastern Gate leads to the old Castle steps. The Black Tower, a Romanesque structure dating to the 12th century which was once used as a prison is next to the Eastern Gate. Opposite the Lobkowicz Palace is the former Castle administration building. In 1960 it was reconstructed and became the House of Czecho-slovak Children.

Running parallel to Jiřská Street from the White Tower to Daliborka Tower is the Golden Lane. Its small, colourful houses are an attraction.

Vikárská Street runs from St. George's Square to the

The Eastern Gate.

northern side of St. Vitus Cathedral. It takes its name from vicars who lived in the street's Old Vicary (Stará Vikárka) which has since been demolished. The most significant building on the street is No. 37, the Old Dean's Palace, with its Baroque facade dating from 1705. The former library, with ceiling frescoes by Vodňanský, on the ground floor is now the Information Office.

Further along the street is the Vikárka restaurant, under which are the ruins of a Romanesque capitular monastery. Behind the Vikárka is the Powder Tower (Mihulka), originally an artillery bastion dating to the 15th century. Damaged by a gunpowder explosion in 1649 it served as a workshop of imperial alchemists under Rudolph II, and is now used for exhibition purposes.

Vikárská Street ends at the front of the Cathedral, facing the Second Courtyard. A gate in the northern wing of the Castle in the Second Courtyard leads to the Powder Bridge.

On the upper floors of the northern wing are the Spanish Hall and Rudolph's Gallery. Both were created to house Rudolph's collections. After several renovations and extensive decoration both halls were damaged by the Prussian bombardment in 1757. The halls were last renovated in 1866 specifically for the intended coronation of Franz Joseph I. They are now used for state purposes and are inaccessible to the public.

The Powder Bridge was originally built as a wooden floor bridge on five stone pillars (1535-36). After the fire of 1541 the bridge was rebuilt to connect the Castle with the newly founded Royal Garden.

Opposite the Royal Garden is the former riding hall with a large riding yard, now used for exhibitions. On the southern border of the Castle are the Rajská Zahrada (the Garden of Paradise) and the Zahrada na Valech (the Garden on the Ramparts). The Zahrada na Baště (the Garden on the Bastion) is located on the western end of the Castle. A trumpeter's tower, a large aviary and an open pavilion with a Renaissance ceiling were built in the Garden of Paradise in 1617. The Garden of the Ramparts was created in 1861 and links with the Garden of Paradise.

View of Prague Castle.

The Rose Window.

One of the twin towers of the western facade.

SAINT VITUS CATHEDRAL (CHRÁM SV. VÍTA)

Located in the heart of the Castle, St. Vitus Cathedral is one of Prague's most imposing buildings. The original church of St. Vitus was founded in the 10th century but construction of the current cathedral began in 1344. Work continued through the centuries and St. Vitus was not completed until 1929. With its exquisite Rose Window, imposing facade and chapels, St. Vitus is a treasure trove of ecclesiastical art and architecture.

Prince Wenceslas founded the original Romanesque rotunda around 926. In the 11th century Prince Spytihněv replaced it with a basilica. Remains of the rotunda and basilica are situated below the present cathedral.

Construction of the present building of the cathedral dates back to the reign of Charles IV in 1344. The first generation of architects involved were the Frenchman Matthias of Arras, succeeded by the German architect Peter Parléř, who later influenced Gothic architecture in Prague. Parléř's sons continued the work after his death, but the Hussite Wars put an end to construction. Although the east part of the cathedral was consecrated in 1385, it was not finished until 1929 after a Czech

The facade of St. Vitus
Cathedral.

The southern facade of the Cathedral.

patriotic association undertook the task of completion. St. Vitus Cathedral is 124 metres long, 60 metres wide and 34 metres high.

The cathedral's unique history is portrayed in sculptured scenes on the bronze gates at its western portal. The western facade brings to mind the Notre Dame in Paris. One of its most striking features is the exterior of the Rose Window depicting the creation of the world. On either side of the window are busts of the cathedral's architects.

The cathedral's south facade, decorated with centuries of art is dominated by the southern tower, and the three-arched portico. The bells on the southern tower are of the Renaissance period while the large

The equestrian statue of St. George.

The three-arched portico with the 14th century mosaic.

The Rudolphian clock on the southern tower.

clock dates back to Rudolph's reign. Underneath the clock is a Gothic window decorated with gold-filigreed Renaissance grille-work. Over the portico is a 14th century mosaic created by Venetian masters depicting scenes from the Last Judgement. Also above the portico are figures of Czech patron saints and portraits of Charles IV and one of his queens, Elizabeth of Pomerania. Inside the three arches are examples of 20th century mosaics by M. Foersterová (1939) depicting Adam and Eve and the Crucifixion.

Once inside the cathedral the most impressive features are the main altar, the stained glass windows and the triforium, a walkway above the pillars with a gallery of portrait busts. The stained glass windows were designed by leading Czech artists. The magnificent rosette is by Kysela. The window on the third chapel on

The Gothic window with the gold filigreed grillework.

The main altar.

The Chapel of St. Sigismund (Zigmund).

the left was designed by Alfons Mucha, better known outside Czechoslovakia for his Art Nouveau posters.

In front of the cathedral's main altar is the Habsburg tomb. Built of white marble, the tomb was designed by the Dutch sculptor A. Collins in 1589 for King Ferdinand I, his wife Anna and their son Maximillian II. Behind the altar are the tombs of the princes and kings of the Přemyslid dynasty. Also of interest is the silver tomb of St. John of Nepomuk.

The main nave is surrounded by chapels the most impressive of which is the Chapel of St. Wenceslas, built on the site of the Romanesque rotunda of the 10th century. The frescoes on the walls, decorated with semi-precious stones and gold, portray Christ's Passion and the story of the life of St. Wenceslas. There are also portraits of Vladislav and his wife Anna of Foix-Candale. The neo-Gothic tomb of St. Wenceslas is located in the middle of the chapel. The tomb, chandelier, floor and ornamentation were reconstructed in the 20th century, but Jindřich Parléř's statue of St. Wenceslas as a Gothic knight on the cornice dates to 1373. The chapel's late-Romanesque iron gate is built in the original Gothic

View of the interior of the Cathedral.

The Chapel of St. Wenceslas.

The choir built by B. Wolmut, 1560.

The silver tomb of St. John of Nepomuk.

View of the triforium.

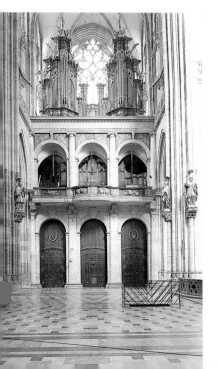

Stained glass windows over the main altar.

Stained glass window decorating
the south side of the Cathedral.

portal. Details from the gate depict the devil pulling out the tongue of Judas and Peter denying Christ.

The choir and the organ are located in the northern part of the transverse nave. The wooden reliefs in the choir are masterpieces of Baroque wood-carving.

A staircase leads to the Treasure chamber directly above St. Wenceslas Chapel. Originally a sacristy, the chamber has housed the Czech crown jewels since 1791. The collection includes St. Wenceslas' gold crown from 1346. The jewels are kept behind seven locks, the seven keys of which are kept by seven separate institutions. The jewels are put on display on special occasions.

A staircase off the main nave leads down to the royal crypt where the remains of the original rotunda of St. Vitus and the basilica of Spytihněv are visible. A number of royals are buried in the crypt including Charles IV, his children and four wives, George of Poděbrady and the daughter of Maria Theresa, Marie Amalie Parmska. The Emperor Rudolph II lies in his original pewter coffin.

The stained glass decoration of the
Rose Window.

Two fine examples of stained glass
decorating St. Vitus Cathedral.

View of the exterior of the Royal Palace.

THE ROYAL PALACE

The Royal Palace, standing on the southeastern side of the Third Courtyard, bears the marks of the many rulers who oversaw its construction from the 10th century on. The remains of the original Romanesque building now lie under the courtyard and can be reached from the ground floor of the palace.

The last important modifications were made in the late fourteenth century by the architect B. Rieth, who was knighted for his achievement. The Palace was home to the Czech kings until the 16th century when the Habsburgs turned it into state offices.

The first three rooms to the left of the Palace entrance constitute the Green Chamber, a former law court and audience hall dating to the 14th century. Further along is an anteroom which housed Vladislav's bedroom and the Land Records Office.

The anteroom leads to the imposing Vladislav's Hall (Vladislavský Sál), named after Vladislav II. The hall 63 metres long, 16 metres wide and 13 metres high has a star-shaped vault and Renaissance windows and was used for coronations and state assemblies. Since 1934 it has been used for presidential elections, national exhibitions, theatre performances and concerts. A terrace to the right offers spellbinding views of Prague.

Near the Vladislav Hall, a staircase leads to the Chapel of All Saints, built by P. Parléř on Romanesque foundations in 1470. The richly decorated chapel was burnt down in 1541, rebuilt between 1579-1580, and connected to Vladislav Hall in 1598. It contains three notable works of art: The Triptych of the Angels by Hans von Aachen, All Saints by Reiner and a cycle of paintings by Dittman. Dittman's work portrays scenes from the life of St. Procopius who is buried in the chapel.

The Bohemian Chancellery, seat of the Bohemian government for hundreds of years, is situated in the Louis wing to the right of Vladislav Hall. It was from one of the rooms in the Chancellery that in 1618 two Catholic governors and a clerk were thrown out of a window for defying a decree guaranteeing freedom of religion to the Bohemian nobility. Although all three survived, (two obelisks in the garden mark the place where the governors fell) the defenestration sparked off the Bohemian rebellion and the Thirty Year's War.

A spiral staircase from an antechamber of the Bohemian Chancellery leads to the hall of the Imperial Court Council, which assembled here under Rudolph II.

The Rider's Staircase, designed for horses, leads out of the most recent part of the Palace into St. George's Square. The staircase was used as an entrance to Vladislav Hall on horseback.

Vladislav Hall.

The Chapel of All Saints.

The room of the new land rolls.

The assembly room.

The twin towers of St. George's Basilica.

ST. GEORGE'S BASILICA

The Church of St. George, founded by Prince Vratislav in 921 is the oldest surviving church in the city. Together with the adjoining convent, the basilica formed the centre of the castle complex in the Middle Ages.

After a fire in 1142 the church was rebuilt in the Romanesque style with two towers, an eastern and western chorus and a crypt. The church underwent large-scale reconstruction in 1897-1907 which gave it its current appearance. Excavations after 1945 revealed the foundations of the old church.

The facade features a relief of St. George, statues of Vratislav and the abbess Mlada who founded the Convent of St. George next to the church.

In the interior of the church are tombs of Přemyslid princes. To the right of the altar is the 15th century painted wooden tomb of Prince Vratislav, in the centre the tomb of Boleslav II and on the left the tomb of Oldřich.

To the right of the choir Ludmilla Chapel is visible though a metal screen.

Detail of the portal on the southern facade.

General view of the interior.

Two views of the crypt.

General view of the interior.

THE HOLY CROSS CHAPEL

The Holy Cross Chapel is situated by the Castle's southern wing in the Second Courtyard. The chapel was built in 1756-1763 by Lurago and renovated in about 1854 when the interior was also redecorated in the neo-Baroque style. Dating to this time are the paintings by Kandler and Navrátil on the walls and vaults. The paintings depict scenes from the Old and New Testaments. The statues on the main altar are by Platzer and the altar's main painting, the Crucifixion, is by Balko. Since 1961 the Holy Cross Chapel has housed ecclesiastical treasures from St. Vitus Cathedral and a collection of valuable works of art, some of which date to the eighth century. The most notable items in the treasury are the Crown Cross, the Old Cross of Záviš, reliquaries and the cassock of St. Wenceslas. The chapel also contains busts of St. Vitus, St. Wenceslas and Vojtěch and chalices from the Baroque period.

The exterior of the Holy Cross Chapel.

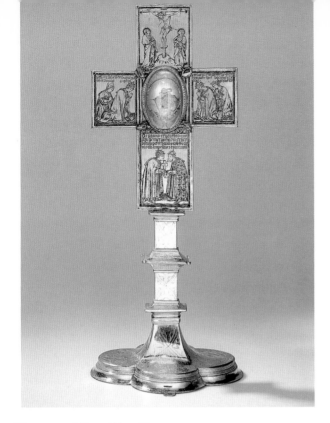

The cross of Pope Urban V.

A jewellery box.

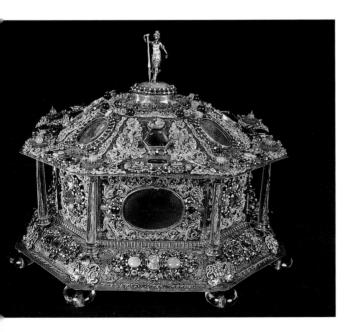

The cross of Záviš.

"The Crucifixion" by a Czech master c. 1390.

General view of the interior of the Bohemian Art Gallery.

THE CONVENT OF ST. GEORGE - BOHEMIAN ART GALLERY

The Convent of St. George, the first Benedictine convent in Bohemia, was founded in 973 by Mlada, sister of Prince Boleslav II, as part of the basilica of St. George. The cross corridor of the convent was built in the 14th century and the convent was rebuilt several times. An extensive complex of buildings with two courtyards was added in the 15th century. The convent was dissolved under Joseph II in 1782 and converted into barracks. In the 1960s it was adapted to house the Bohemian Art Gallery. It contains valuable collections of Czech art from the Gothic to the Baroque periods. Important works include paintings by artists who took part in the construction of many of Prague's churches.

"The Birth of St. Wenceslas" by K. Škréta, 1641.

"St. Elisabeth" by master Theodorik,
late 14th century.

"The Assumption" by a Czech master, c.1450.

"St. Vojtěch" by Jan Očko, c. 1371.

Two general views of the interior of the Picture Gallery.

THE PRAGUE CASTLE PICTURE GALLERY

The Gallery is situated on the ground floor of the northern and western wings of the Castle in the Second Courtyard. The original collection was largely put together by Rudolph II who was a great patron of the arts. Although the original Rudolphian collection was seized by the Swedes during the 1648 occupation, works by Bartolomej Spranger, Hans van Aachen and others serve as a reminder of how important it was. Ferdinand III (1637-1657) renewed the collection by acquiring works from auctions and private collections. Among these were many outstanding works from the Italian, German, Dutch, Flemish and Czech schools. Under Charles VI, however, paintings were systematically sold off. In the 1960s art historians identified paintings of well-known masters among the remaining works and a selection of them are on display in the gallery. They include works by Tizian, Veronese, Rubens, Tintoretto, Kupecký and Brandl.

"The Apostle Paul" by P. Brandl, c. 1725.

"A Young Woman" by Tizian Vecellio, c. 1515.

"Shepherds Adoring Jesus" by J. Robusti (Tintoretto).

View of Lobkowicz Palace and the eastern part of Prague Castle.

View of one of the exhibition halls.

Three views of the interior of Lobkowicz Palace.

THE PALACE OF LOBKOWICZ

The palace was built in the 16th century by Vratislav of Pernstejn. Its present appearance dates to 1651 when it was rebuilt by Euseb of Lobkowicz according to a plan by Lurago. Most of the interior has been preserved, but the exterior dates from 1791. The palace was owned by the Lobkowicz family until the 20th century. The stucco work on the ceiling of the first floor is by Galli and the paintings by Harovník. The Chapel of the Holy Trinity with scenes from the life of St. Wenceslas is located in the northern wing. In 1973 the palace was reconstructed and is now a section of the National Museum devoted to Czech history.

General view of the Golden Lane.

THE GOLDEN LANE

This lane of tiny, colourful houses, built into the arches of the Rudolphian wall, is one of the most picturesque areas of Prague. Completed in the second half of the 16th century between the White Tower and the Daliborka Tower, the houses originally provided accommodation to archers defending the Palace. It was later inhabited by artisans including goldsmiths who gave the street its name. According to a 19th century legend it was from here that the alchemists from Rudolph's court tried to discover the secret of eternal life and how to make gold. In the 18th and 19th century the houses were inhabited by the poor. Later on many writers lived here. The most famous among them were Franz Kafka who lived at No. 22 and the Nobel laureate, the poet Jaroslav Seifert. Today most of the houses are souvenir shops.

Detail of a house in the Golden Lane.

Views of the Golden Lane.

General view of the Royal Garden.

The entrance to the Royal Garden.

THE ROYAL GARDEN

The Royal Garden was founded by Ferdinand I in 1534. The original garden was the work of G. Spatio and the horticulturist Francesco and many exotic plants were cultivated here. After suffering damage during the Thirty Year's War it underwent renovation. A new addition was the fountain with its statue of Hercules by Bendl (1670) in a Baroque niche opposite the Summer Palace. In the early 18th century, under the architect Dienzenhofer, it took on the appearance of a Baroque garden. It was considerably damaged by the French in 1743 and totally destroyed by Prussian artillery in 1757. In the 19th century the garden was converted into an English park but fell into neglect. It was brought to life again after 1918 by the architect Janák who reconstructed the original Renaissance garden in front of the Summer Palace and repaired the Singing Fountain, built between 1564-1568 by Tomáš Jaroš.

On the northwestern edge of the garden is the former

Views of the Royal Garden.

zoo, called the Lví Dvorek (The Lions' Yard), where wild animals, including lions, tigers and bears were kept until 1740. To the right of the entrance is the house of the former royal gardener, built in 1572.

The Summer Palace on the eastern edge of the garden is one of the finest examples of Italian Renaissance architecture outside Italy. It was designed in the 16th century by architect Paolo della Stella and built by Italian masters Maria dal Pambio and G. Spatio. The 74 reliefs in the arcaded gallery around the palace, depicting historical events and mythological themes are by Paolo della Stella. In 1841-1855 the Palace was converted into a picture gallery and today serves as an exhibition hall.

Another interesting building is the Ball Room designed by Wolmut in 1569 and rebuilt by P. Janák in 1946-1950. Its original ornamental sgraffiti, carefully restored, are an immediate eye catcher. Important international and political meetings are often held here today.

St. George's Square.

Rožmberk Palace in St. George's Square.

Vikárská Street.

The street leading to
the Golden Lane.

Jiřská Street.

Two views of Hradčany Square.

HRADČANY SQUARE

Situated on the western end of Prague Castle is Hradčany Square. Hradčany was founded around the year 1320 by the Castle administrator as a tributary town. Walls were constructed around the area in the reign of Charles IV and the entry gates were in Kanovnická and Loretánská Streets. In 1375, Aleš of Malkovice, the provincial governor, extended it by adding Pohořelec, Nový Svět and Úvoz.

In the period of the Hussite wars the area was burnt down and following the construction of nobles' and cannons' houses in 1541 the area took on its present impressive appearance. In 1598 Hradčany was promoted to a royal town and established its own town hall.

In the southern part of Hradčany Square are two palaces, Salmovský Palace built between 1800-1810 in the Classical style by architect F. Pavlíček, and Schwarzenberg Palace dating back to the 16th century.

Next to it is the monastery of the Barnabites, founded in 1626. After the abolition of the monastery in 1786 the building was given to the Carmelites of St. Joseph in Malá Strana.

Within the monastery complex is the Church of St. Benedict, dating back to 1353. Formerly a parish church of Gothic origin it was rebuilt in 1655 and redecorated in the 17th and 18th centuries.

Opposite the Castle occupying the western part of the square is Tuscany Palace. The four winged building with an inner courtyard was designed by J. B. Matthey in the Baroque style and built in 1689-91 on the site of several older houses. On the outer wall are several statues including an outstanding work of Archangel Michael by O. Most in 1693. The palace was bought by the grand duchess of Tuscany in the 1720's.

On the northern edge of Hradčany Square is Martinic (Martinský) Palace (No. 67) built in the second half of the 16th century on the site of four Gothic houses. The sgraffiti on the court facades date back to 1580s. The palace was enlarged by Jaroslav Bořita of Martinic. In the reconstructed northern wing is a large hall. Adjoining it is a chapel with wall paintings dating back to the turn

The facade of the Archbishop's Palace.

of the 17th century. Other rooms have painted beam ceilings. The building was reconstructed in 1973 and now serves as the home of Prague's chief architect.

Further along close to the main gate of Prague Castle is the Archbishop's Palace (No. 56), originally built in the early 16th century as a Renaissance palace and renovated several times. The latest renovation was in 1764-1765 when architect J. J. Wirch gave it a late Baroque character. The balcony portal at the entrance and the roof pavilion were designed by J. B. Matthey around 1675-1679. There is a stucco decorated chapel inside with busts of St. Peter and St. Paul, dating back to 1413. The palace also boasts a unique set of eight Gobelin tapestries with motifs of the New Indies of the mid 18th century.

Through the nearby lane next to the palace is Šternberk (Šternberský) Palace (No. 57) a Baroque four-wing building designed by Václav Vojtěch, the Earl of Šternberk and built between 1698-1707. It now houses the collection of European art of the National Gallery.

Situated in the centre of Hradčany Square is a statue of Our Lady and eight saints, created by F. M. Brokof in 1726.

The principal street of Hradčany is Loreta (Loretá-nská) Street leading towards Loretánské Square. At the top of the street is the former Hradčany town hall (No. 173), a Renaissance two-wing building with a sgraffito facade, built around 1603. On the opposite side is the

Tuscany Palace.

The richly decorated facade of Martinic Palace.

new Martinic Palace (No. 181) designed by B. Scotti and built between 1702-1705. Farther on is Hržan (Hržanský) Palace (No. 177) originally a Gothic house belonging to Peter Parléř. It was adapted to the Renaissance style in the second half of the 16th century and rebuilt in the late Baroque style in the late 18th century. It is now used by the Federal government.

In the eastern part of Loretánské Square is the Loreta chapel and on the northern side is the oldest Capuchin monastery of Bohemia, (No. 99) dating back to the beginning of the 17th century connected to the Church of Our Lady. On the western part of the square is Černín (Černínský) Palace, an early Baroque monumental two floor building, constructed between 1668-1697 on the site of several old houses by Humprecht Černín of Chudenic, the emperor's ambassador to Venice. The interior of the palace was rebuilt in the early 18th century, and in the second half of the 19th century the palace served as army barracks. Since 1928 it has housed the Ministry of Foreign Affairs.

Close by is Strahov monastery with its churches and impressive library.

Černín Palace.

General view of the northern side of Hradčany Square.

Loreta Street.

"The Virgin Mary, Baby Jesus, Zacharias, Elisabeth and Baby John the Baptist" by V. Catena, c. 1517.

General view of the interior of the art gallery.

"Jesus" by El Greco, c. 1590.

"The Rosary Feast" by A. Dürer, 1506.

ŠTERNBERK PALACE - COLLECTION OF EUROPEAN ART

The Baroque building houses the collection of European art of the National Gallery. On the ground floor is a collection of 19th century French art and sculpture, as well as French realist, impressionist and modern paintings. On the first floor exhibits include a collection of icons and Italian paintings from the 14th to the 18th centuries, including Tintoretto, Bronzino, Guido Reni and Canaletto. Dutch artists are represented by Halls, Rembrandt, and Van Ostade. On the second floor exhibits include works by Poussin, Mignard, Fragonard and Boucher, the Spanish painters El Greco, Murillo, Riber and Goya and the German artists L. Cranach, Holbein, and Dürer. Also exhibited on the second floor are works by Breughel, Rubens and 19th and 20th century Russian, German, Austrian, Italian, Spanish and Norwegian artists.

"Don Miguel de Lardizaba" by Goya, 1815.

The facade of Schwarzenberg Palace.

SCHWARZENBERG PALACE - MUSEUM OF MILITARY HISTORY

Designed by architect Galli Vlach at around 1562 and built on the site of four noble houses, Schwarzenberg Palace belonged first to Jan of Lobkovice but takes its name from the Schwarzenbergs who acquired it in 1719.

One of the most important buildings of the Czech Renaissance style with imposing shields, cornices, and sgraffito, it now houses a military museum.

The exterior of the building is richly decorated with exquisite sgraffito based on Italian models dating back to 1562 and repaired twice, first in the late 19th and again in the mid 20th century.

Its interior is equally impressive with painted panel ceilings and exhibits a fine collection of weapons, flags and other items of military history. In the courtyard is a fine array of cannons.

View of the Inner Courtyard.

General view of the interior of the Military Museum.

Details of exhibits.

The facade of the Loreto.

THE LORETO (LORETA)

Situated on the eastern side of Loretánské Square is the Loreto with its impressive Baroque facade dominated by a bell tower. Loreto is famous for its Santa Casa, a copy of the Italian shrine of Loreto, which according to tradition is the house of the Virgin Mary. On both sides of the Santa Casa are two fountains from the 1740s by J. M. Bruder and R. Prachner. It is surrounded by cloisters, chapels and the Church of the Nativity of Our Lord. This former pilgrimage place was built in 1626 and expanded over the years. Stucco decorations were added to the exterior in 1664 while the ground floor cloisters, designed by G. B. Orsi were built in the same year. A second floor was added to the cloisters by K. L. Dienzenhofer in 1746.

The paintings of the vault of the nave in the Church of the Nativity are by J. A. Schopf while the paintings in the vault of the presbytery are by V. V. Reiner. Several artists namely P. Brandl, F. A. Schefler, M. Schönherr, M. V. Jackel and R. Prachner were involved in the decoration of the church and chapel. On the tower, built in 1693 is the famous carillon of 27 bells by P. Neumann of 1694. Statues by Quitainer and Kohl decorate the balustrade.

The Loreto treasury, situated on the first floor, houses a collection of 16th to 19th century treasures including a Gothic chalice from 1510, religious gowns and jewellery, as well as a famous 12 kilogram (golden) silver monstrance (receptacle) embedded with 6222 diamonds dating back to 1698.

The interior of the
Santa Casa.

The exterior of the
Santa Casa.

The Strahov evangelistary on parchment paper, 9th century.

View of Strahov Monastery.

STRAHOV MONASTERY

Founded by Prince Vladislav II around 1140 at the instigation of Jindřich Zdik, Bishop of Olomouc, on Hradčany overlooking Prague, Strahov monastery was expanded and reconstructed through the centuries. The oldest Premonstratensian monastery in Bohemia, it now boasts one of the most important libraries in the country.

The complex, with four courtyards, includes the Church of Our Lady, the Church of St. Roch and retains the original Romanesque wall. The monastery quickly gained a reputation as one of the most significant centres of education in the country, and owes much of its fame to its library. Its religious significance increased even further when the relics of Saint Norbert were brought here from Magdeburg in 1627. There is a statue of the saint by J. A. Quitainer (1742) at the gate.

The main courtyard is surrounded by buildings including the wing with the office of the former General Provisor. The monastery was housed in a four-wing building around the Courtyard of Paradise, built from 1142 to 1182 and rebuilt in the early Baroque and mid-Renaissance styles. A separate building, the Philosophical Hall, was built between 1782 and 1784. Designed by I. J. Pallardi it has a ceiling fresco depicting the History of the Species by F. A. Maulbertsch of 1794. A wing joins the monastery with the Theological Hall, built between 1671-1679 by J. D. Orsi. The paintings are

The Theological Hall.

The Philosophical Hall.

by Siard Nosecky. The Baroque shelves display theological literature and there are several 17th and 18th century globes. The glass cases have numerous illuminated manuscripts and incunabula, (books printed in movable type) dating from before the 16th century. The oldest manuscript is a pergameneous (parchment) evangelistary (the four Gospels) from the ninth century.

The Church of Our Lady is actually a Romanesque building completed by 1182 but reconstructed several times through the centuries. The 17th century vault is decorated with frescoes by J. Kramolín, I. Raab and J. V. Neuherz. The current appearance dates back to

1743-1752 when A. Lurago oversaw the renovation of the two towers and decorated the facade with statues by J. A. Quitainer. The interior, the paintings and the sculpture of the church are the works of leading Baroque artists of the period while the church houses the organ on which Mozart played, built in 1746.

The Church of St. Roch, situated near the gate, is a Gothic Renaissance central building with three polygonal sides founded by Rudolph II in 1599. When the reconstruction of the monastery was completed in 1953 a garden was opened under the southern church wing on the hill.

View of Malá Strana from Charles Bridge.

MALÁ STRANA --
THE LESSER QUARTER

Built below Prague Castle, on the left bank of the river Vltava, with its Baroque character, Malá Strana is the second oldest part of the city. The imposing palaces, churches and monasteries make it one of the most attractive quarters of the city and an architectural gem.

Its origins go back to the ninth and 10th centuries but the street plan dates from the 13th century when King Otakar II encouraged new colonists, primarily Germans, to settle in the area. In the 14th century Charles IV enlarged and added new fortifications to the area which became known as the Lesser Town of Prague.

Almost every building from the early days, however, was destroyed in the Hussite wars and series of fires in the Middle Ages. The district was rebuilt in the Renaissance style and later in the 17th and 18th centuries took on a Baroque character. When the nobility moved back to Vienna in the late 18th century Malá Strana was inhabited by officials and poorer citizens. This put an end to the construction boom, and allowed Malá Strana to retain its Baroque character.

After the unification of Prague in 1784 the Lesser Town ceased to be a separate town and became one of the quarters of Prague.

The Town Square, where markets were held for centuries, is in the centre of Malá Strana. The original market was separated by the Church of St. Nicholas into an upper and lower square. Next to it is the former Jesuit college which now serves as the Mathematics and Physics faculty of Charles University. In the square is the Plague Column, a monument sponsored by the survivors of the 1715 epidemic.

Opposite the Church of St. Nicholas is Lichtenstein Palace. Reconstructed from five Renaissance buildings it takes up the whole western side of the upper part of the square. The palace dates to the late 14th century but was rebuilt in 1791 by the Lichtensteins when architect M. Hummel gave the former Renaissance buildings their neo-Classical facade.

Also visible from St. Nicholas Church is the Golden Lion House, one of the few original Renaissance houses in the Malá Strana.

The lower side of the square is bordered on the right by the Palais Kaiserstein where the opera singer Emmy Destinova lived. On the left side is the former town hall.

There are five main streets leading from the square: Letenská, Tomášská, Nerudova, Karmelitskà and Mostecká.

Letenská Street, with its many palaces leads to Wallenstein Garden, open to the public from May to September.

At the entrance of Letenská Street from the square is St. Thomas Church, one of Prague's most notable churches. The adjoining Augustinian monastery was founded by King Wenceslas II in 1285, and the monastery building and Gothic church were built between 1285 and 1316. Heavily damaged by fire several times the monastery still retains the Chapel of St. Barbara. It now serves as a home for the elderly.

The church suffered heavily in a fire and in 1723 was rebuilt by Dienzenhofer. Some of the original details including the Renaissance portal were saved. The ceiling frescoes are by V.V. Reiner and date back to 1728-1730. On the altar are copies of P. Rubens' paintings of St. Thomas and St. Augustine. The originals are now in the National Gallery.

Tomášská Street with the House of the Golden Stag, (No. 26) leads to Wallenstein Square, dominated by Wallenstein Palace, built on the site of 23 Renaissance

General view of Malá Strana.

houses. Facing it is Leebour Palace (No. 162).

Nerudova Street climbs up to Prague Castle, the entrance of which was through the Strakoviska Gate. Named after Jan Neruda, the Czech poet and journalist of the last century, the street is lined with important houses and palaces. They include Morzinský Palace, (No. 256) the house of B. Spranger, King Rudolph II's painter (No. 209) and Thun-Hohenstenstein Palace (No. 214), an impressive Baroque building with a portal and heraldic eagles by M.B. Braun.

Also on Nerudova Street is the Church of our Lady built in 1717 and Bretfeld Palace (No. 240), a Rococo structure by J.J. Wirch where famous balls with Casanova and Mozart on the guest list were held. Also worth mentioning is the reconstructed Renaissance house (No. 233) which still retains its original Renaissance portal where Jan Neruda once lived.

Karmelitská Street leads westerly from the Town Square. Enclosed between Karmelitská Street and the Vltava is one of Malá Strana's most picturesque areas and Kampa Island. Situated in Karmelitská Street is the Church of Our Lady Victorious, built by Lutherans in 1613. It became the property of Carmelites in 1624, who built a monastery and renovated the church. On the central altar is the renowned wax figure of "Bambino di Praga" (Prague's Infant Jesus), a gift from Spain. A Carmelite cemetery is located under the church. The building became a parish church in 1784.

No. 388 was originally the Convent of St. Mary Magdalene dating to the 14th century. It was demolished during the Hussite period, but some of the original masonry has been preserved. In 1677 the building was rebuilt into a Dominican monastery and church. In 1783 the monastery and the church were abolished. The building later served as a post office and barracks. Today it is the State Central Archives office.

Rohan Palace (No. 386), was built in 1796 on the site of three houses. The original plan was by J. Zobel; subsequent owners and their architects have made considerable changes. The rear part of the palace reaches as far as Maltese Square.

Karmelitská Street leads to Újezd Street, where Michna Palace (No. 450), is located. The palace is now a sports museum. In Újezd Street is the terminal of the funicular leading to Petřín Hill.

Near the beginning of Karmelitská Street is Prokopská Street which leads to Lázeňská Street, site of several important buildings. They include the Convent of the Order of the Maltese Knights, the Church of Our Lady Below the Chain, originally a 12th century basilica belonging to the Knights of Malta and the House at the Baths, which housed the town baths in the 14th century. The House at the Baths later served as a prominent Prague hotel. Peter the Great, the French writer Chateaubriand and the French aviator Blanchard were among its guests.

Lázeňská Street leads to the Maltese Square with its sculpture of John the Baptist by Brokoff. The Baroque palaces facing the square now house a library, the Museum of Musical Instruments and the Japanese Embassy.

Nearby a small bridge connects the square with Kampa Island. Its park was created by joining the gardens of the former palaces. This picturesque site also offers a beautiful view of the Old Town. A group of houses on the waterfront is known as the "Venice of Prague". The first reference to the island dates back to 1169, when it was referred to as the lower island. A flight of steps from Kampa Island leads to Charles Bridge.

From the Town Square Mostecká Street, the narrow shopping street lined with Baroque houses, leads to Charles Bridge.

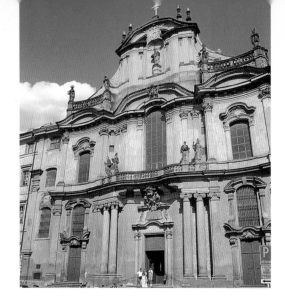

View of the facade of St. Nicholas Church.

THE CHURCH OF ST. NICHOLAS

St. Nicholas is Prague's greatest Baroque church. Its huge dome and bell tower which are 79 metres high are among Prague's best known landmarks. It is the work of Bavarian architect C. Dientzenhofer, his son Kilian and the architect A. Lurago.

The site of the present church was originally occupied by a Gothic church dating to the 13th century. In 1625 the Emperor Ferdinand II gave the church to the Jesuit order. C. Dientzenhofer built a new church in the early 18th century. The work was continued by his son, who added the dome, and completed by Lurago in 1755 with the erection of the bell tower. Soon after the church was built, the Jesuit order was dissolved by Pope Clement XIV. Since then St. Nicholas has been used as a parish church.

Its impressive and richly decorated interior is the work of some of the most acclaimed Baroque artists. The ceiling fresco by J. L. Kracker is one of the largest frescoes in Europe, covering 1,500 square metres and depicting scenes from the life of St. Nicholas. The fresco inside the cupola is the work of F. X. Palko. The wooden stucco statues by the pillars in the nave, the four large statues of saints below the dome and the statue of St. Nicholas on the high altar are the work of I. F. Platzer. Other notable works of art in the church are: the Holy Cross by Škréta, St. Barbara by L. Kohl, St. Michael by F. Solimena and the Death of St. Francis by F.X. Balko.

A detail of the interior of St. Nicholas Church.
The cupola.

The main
altar.

General view of Wallenstein Gardens.

WALLENSTEIN GARDENS

Wallenstein Gardens were created in the 17th century as part of Wallenstein Palace, residence of general Albrecht von Wallenstein whose dramatic life inspired Schiller to write his famous play. The gardens are a testimony to Wallenstein's political aspirations. He installed an artificial grotto, an aviary and a triple arched loggia (sala terrena) designed by Pieroni. The loggia is richly decorated with frescoes; the ceiling stucco work and paintings are the work of Bianco. The loggia today is often used for concerts and plays during the summer months.

The main path in the gardens is lined with bronze statues of mythological gods and goddesses by Adrien de Vries, copies of those taken to Sweden during the Thirty Year's War. The sculpture of Hercules, gracing the pond is also a Vries copy.

Opposite the loggia is the Wallenstein riding school. Its hall now serves as an exhibition area for the National Gallery.

View of the loggia.

The funicular connecting Malá Strana with Petřín Hill.

PETŘÍN HILL

Petřín hill, situated 318 metres above sea level not only offers a spellbinding view of Prague but is an interesting park in its own right. It can be reached from Újezd Street in Malá Strana by funicular. The 63.5 metre high Petřín lookout tower on the top of the hill, built in 1891 for Prague's Jubilee Exhibition, is a copy of the Eiffel tower. Nearby is the labyrinth of mirrors also built in 1891. It leads to a gallery with paintings of the battle of 1684 between the inhabitants of Prague and Swedish troops on Charles Bridge by K. and L. Liebscher and V. Bartoněk.

The Church of St. Vavřinec (St. Lawrence) built in 1135 was originally a one nave Romanesque church. It took on its present Baroque appearance after restoration work in 1735 and 1740 and again in 1770. Only four years later the church was abolished but reopened in 1830. Inside on the altar there is a painting of the torture of St. Vavřinec by J. C. Monna from 1693, repainted by V. Makovský in 1840. Near the church is the Chapel of the Tomb of Christ built in 1732. The Calvary Chapel was built around the same time.

Leading down one side of the hill are the remains of the Hunger Wall, built under Charles IV to serve as the fortifications of Malá Strana. It is believed that Charles ordered the wall to be built in order to provide employment for the poor inhabitants of Prague, hence its name.

Petřín is also a popular park with Prague's citizens, with restaurants and look-out posts which can be reached either on foot, or by the funicular.

The Calvary Chapel on Petřín Hill.

The Petřín look-out tower.

St. Thomas Church.

The Church of Our Lady Below the Chain.

Steps connecting Malá Strana with Hradčany.

View of St. Nicholas Church.

Views of Nerudova Street.

Two views of Malá Strana.

Views of Kampa Island.

An artist at work on Charles Bridge.

General view of Charles Bridge.

CHARLES BRIDGE

Charles Bridge a major landmark of Prague, connects Malá Strana with Staré Město across the River Vltava. Historically it has been inextricably linked with the development of Prague. It holds a special place in the heart of town people and visitors alike for its colourful and lively "bridge life", imbuing it with an atmosphere reminiscent of Montmartre in Paris. The bridge is a popular haunt for artists and buskers, who, taking up positions under the numerous statues, vie for the attention of passers by.

The original wooden bridge, the oldest on the river, near where the Charles Bridge is now, was built in 935 and repaired in 1118. Queen Judith ordered the first stone bridge to be built in 1170. The bridge which took her name was destroyed during the flood of 1342. The smaller bridge tower was preserved but the second one with a gate was incorporated into the Church of the Knights of the Cross.

The present stone bridge was built of sandstone by the Parléř workshop in the reign of Charles IV between 1357 and 1402, and was originally called Stone or Prague Bridge. It took the name Charles in 1870. It is 515 metres long and 9.5 metres wide with 16 arches. Through the centuries it has withstood several floods

Views of Charles Bridge.

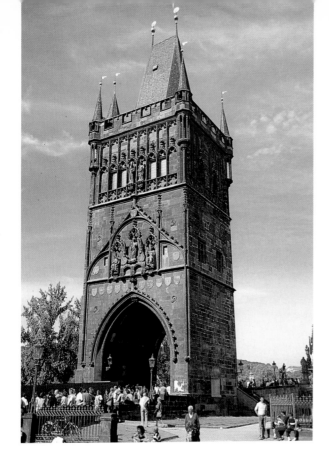

The Staré Město bridge gate.

The Malá Strana bridge gate.

most notably in 1432, 1655, 1784 and 1890. Following renovation in 1974, road traffic was banned and the bridge was restricted to pedestrians.

On the Malá Strana bank is the bridge gate with two towers. The smaller one, of Romanesque origin, was built from blocks of stone in about 1170 and belonged to Judith's Bridge. On the tower there is a Romanesque relief depicting the sovereign on the throne and a youngster kneeling. The second tower was built in 1464 in a style similar to the Staré Město tower, but has no sculptures.

The bridge has 30 statues, 15 on each side installed as from 1683 and commissioned by churches, the university, the town council and individuals. These account for its description as an open air statue gallery. Many of the statues are now copies, the originals having been moved to the museums. The most important is the

Dream of St. Luitgard by M. B. Braun dating back to 1710. The oldest statue is that of St. John of Nepomuk honouring the saint who was thrown over the bridge into the river.

The tower on the Staré Město bank, one of the most beautiful gateways in Europe, served as part of the fortifications of the bridge. Built towards the end of 14th and the beginning of the 15th centuries by Peter Parléř it still retains its imposing decorations. They include the coat of arms of Charles IV and the signs of the kingfisher over the gate, and the statues of St. Vitus, patron of the bridge on the first floor. On the second floor are copies of the original statues of St. Vojtěch and St. Sigismund (Zigmund). The western part of the tower was damaged during the battles of 1648 and 1848. There is also a commemorative plaque marking the successful defence of Staré Město against the Swedes.

Three of the statues decorating Charles Bridge.

View of the Old Town.

THE OLD TOWN - STARÉ MĚSTO

This picturesque district of Prague, with its cobbled stone streets, remarkable variety of old houses and important churches retains all the character and charm of its glorious past.

The origins of the Old Town go back to the 10th century when settlement centered round the ford of the river, crossing point of three important trade routes.

The area quickly prospered. A thriving market developed probably as early as the end of the 11th century on the site of today's Old Town Square and by the 12th century the community was firmly established. In the 13th century, under King Wenceslas, the Old Town received city rights and was fortified with a series of moats.

But the construction of the New Town in 1348 put a barrier to further expansion, enclosing the Old Town between the New Town and the River Vltava.

The centre of the Old Town is the monumental Old Town Square and the most important streets leading out of the square are Karlova, Celetná and Pařížská.

Křížovnické Square, with the statue of Charles IV by A. Hahnel, stands at the Old Town end of Charles Bridge. At the northern end of the square is the Church of St. Francis and the Monastery of the Knights of the Cross with a Red Star. The order was founded by Anne, daughter of Wenceslas I. It was entrusted with maintaining the bridge and collecting taxes and tolls from people crossing it. The Baroque Church of St. Francis was built between 1679-1689 over the Church of the Holy Ghost, remains of which can be seen in the crypt.

Close by on the Smetana embankment is the Smetana Museum. This neo-Renaissance building built between 1876-1884 once served as the municipal waterworks. Its facade is decorated with sgraffito work by J. Subic. Nearby is a tower with a clock, built in the second half of the 16th century.

Opposite Křížovnické Square is the Clementinum, a former Jesuit college which now serves as a state library. This complex of buildings with its many courtyards is the second largest in Prague after Hradčany. It was built in 1556 on the site of 32 houses, a monastery, two gardens and three churches. On the abolition of the Jesuit order in 1773, it became the property of the University of Prague and in 1928 became the seat of the state library.

Of special interest is the 18th century astronomical tower, the Mirror Chapel in the fourth courtyard decorated with stucco work embedded with mirrors, and Mozart's Hall with rococo wall paintings, situated on the first floor of the west wing.

Opposite Charles Bridge on Karlova Street is the Church of St. Salvator, built as a triple nave building with a cupola and two towers.

Karlova Street, a twisted cobbled stone road lined with magnificent buildings, links Charles Bridge with the Lesser Square which leads to the Old Town Square. On the right hand side close to the river is the Colloredo-Mansfield Palace (No. 189) an 18th century Baroque four wing building. Further along is the House at the French Crown (No. 188). Built at the turn of the 17th century it was the home of famous astronomer Johannes Kepler from 1607 to 1612. Potting Palace (No. 186) has a monumental portal and window cornices.

Further along, the House at the Golden Snake (No. 181) served as the first cafe in Prague in 1714. Opposite is the Church of St. Clement with a simple exterior and a lavishly decorated interior, including frescoes and sculptures. It now serves as a Greek Catholic church.

Further along Karlova Street at the intersection with Jilská Street, is the Church of St. Giles built in the 14th century on the site of an older church and later redecorated in the Baroque style.

Karlova Street leads on to the Lesser Square (Malé náměstí) graced by a public fountain with an imposing Renaissance grille dating back to 1560 and lined with several interesting houses. The most notable of these are the House at the White Lion (No. 143) with its late Gothic portal and the House at the Three White Roses (No. 142) richly decorated with paintings by M. Aleš.

The Lesser Square leads on to the Old Town Square, a treasure trove of fine buildings, not least the Old Town Hall with its tower and astronomical clock.

From the northern side of the Old Town Square, Pařížská Avenue lined with shops and offices, goes past the Jewish Town and on to the Vltava embankment.

From the east end of the Old Town Square, Celetná Street, one of the oldest is Prague, leads to the Black Powder Tower. Lined with stone houses dating as far back as the 13th century, Celetná is a pedestrian street and once formed part of the Royal Way. The most notable building is the House of the Black Mother of God, a cubist style building which takes its name from the small statue in a corner niche. Opposite is the former mint.

Close to Celetná Street, on Malá Štuparstká Street is the Church of St. Jacob.

From the Old Town Square Železná Street leads to the Tyl Theatre, located in the area of the Fruit Market. Designed by A. Haffnecker and built in 1781 by Count F. A. Nostic-Rhienek, its interior was decorated by J. Q. Jahn. The first performance was in 1783 while the world premier of Mozart's Don Giovanni was performed here in 1787.

Opposite the Tyl Theatre is the Carolinum, the main building of Charles University, Central Europe's oldest university which was founded in 1348. At first the university did not have its own building. The Carolinum, adapted from a Gothic house was given to Charles College by Wenceslas IV in 1383. Through the years other adjoining buildings were incorporated into the Carolinum which was reconstructed in the Baroque style in 1718. The latest renovation took place in the 1960s.

The university was one of the centres of the Hussites; its preachers included Jan Huss. Following the defeat of the Hussites at the Battle of the White Mountain in 1620 the university was taken over by the Jesuits. In 1881 the university was divided into two schools -- one using Czech and the other German.

Other places of interest in the Old Town include: the Convent of St. Agnes in Anežská Street, which houses an important art collection, Bethlehem Chapel in Bethlehem Square where Jan Huss preached from 1371 to 1415, and the Rudolphinum or House of Artists in Jan Palach Square. The square is named after the student who burnt himself to death after the 1968 invasion of Czechoslovakia. The Rudolphinum, an outstanding neo-Renaissance building which served as the National Assembly building during the First Republic, is now an important concert hall.

Almost every street and square of the Old Town is a testimony to a rich historical past -- whether it be the remains of the fortifications, the cobbled stone streets or the distinct houses. Many of these grace the squares which have replaced old markets such as the egg and coal markets. Best explored on foot, the Old Town is a voyage into history.

General view of the Old Town Square.

THE OLD TOWN SQUARE

The Old Town Square belies its humble origins as a 12th century market place surrounded by houses. Through the centuries it was witness to crucial events in Prague's history including the execution in the 17th century of the leaders of the Battle of the White Mountain. The square was a major stop in coronation processions and venue for numerous celebrations and demonstrations.

The Old Town Square, a hub of life, offers not only size but variety, and can claim to concentrate some of the most interesting buildings of Prague, not least the Town Hall from which the square takes its name, St. Nicholas to the north and Týn Church to the west. A web of cobbled narrow streets lined with beautiful old houses lead off the square.

In the middle of the square is the imposing statue of John Huss, by L. Šaloun, erected in 1915 on the 500th anniversary of his death at the stake.

The Church of Our Lady of Týn.

The statue of John Huss.

View of the northern part of the square.

On the northern side of the square is the former Pauline monastery (No. 930) with its sculpture by M. V. Jackel (1696) on the gable.

On the western side of the square is the Goltz Kinsky Palace (No. 606) designed by K. I. Dienzenhofer and A. Lurago and built in 1746 by Count J. Goltz. The statues are by F. I. Platzer and the stucco decoration is by C.G. Bossi. The palace was rebuilt in the Classical style for Prince R. Kinsky in 1834. It now houses a collection of the National Gallery, including 150,000 watercolours, drawings and graphics by J. Mánes, M. Aleš and V. Hollan among others.

The adjoining building, the House at the Stone Bell (No. 605) was built in the second half of the 13th century and was rebuilt as a Gothic town palace in the second quarter of the 14th century. At the corner is a sign of a stone bell from which the house takes its name. The wall paintings in the hall on the corner tower date back to the second half of the 14th century. After 1685 the house was redecorated in the Baroque style and the Gothic parts were damaged. In 1889 it was redecorated in the neo-Baroque style. Reconstruction work in the 1980s, restored the house's Gothic style and it now serves as a museum, concert and exhibition hall.

View of the Old Town Hall.

Views of the Old Town Square.

Next to the House at the Stone Bell is the Týn School (No 604) built on the site of two Gothic houses, joined and reconstructed in the Renaissance style at the beginning of the 15th century. The Venetian arch gables from the middle of the 16th century still survive while the pointed lancet windows were revealed under the smooth Classic style plaster after reconstruction work. The building served as a school from 1400 on and famous teachers included architect M. Rejsek. The corner house (No. 603) is of Romanesque origin.

On the southern side of the square is Storch's House (No. 552). The facade of this neo-Renaissance building is decorated with a large painting of St. Wenceslas on horseback by M. Aleš. The House at the Unicorn (No. 548) still retains the remains of the original 12th century Romanesque house in its basement. A tower house was built on top of the original house in the 13th century. In the late 15th century the house was the seat of the Bishop Lucian of Mirandola. The vaulted carriageway, designed by M. Rejsek dates back to 1496. Composer Bedřich Smetana used the house as a music school.

On the corner with Melantrichova Street is the House at the Ox (No. 462) with an early Baroque gable and an original Gothic portal dating back to the beginning of the 15th century.

Storch's House.

The House at the Stone Bell.

Three houses on the southern side of the Old Town Square.

View of the facade of the Old Town Hall.

THE OLD TOWN HALL

The Old Town Hall is one of Prague's most remarkable buildings. It was expanded over the centuries through the incorporation of various houses, the exteriors of which retain their individual characteristics, giving the impression that the complex is several separate buildings. Perhaps the most striking feature of the exterior is the 70 metre high tower, offering spellbinding views of Prague, and the unique astrological clock below it.

The Old Town Hall was built following King John of Luxembourg's decision in 1338 to grant town councillors the privilege of establishing a resident town council.

The House at the Minute.

The astronomical clock.

The 70 m high tower of the Old Town Hall.

A decorated window on the facade of the Old Town Hall.

View of the chapel.

The assembly hall.

They bought Wolflin's house and gradually incorporated houses in the immediate vicinity. A porch and chapel were added in the eastern side in 1348 while a council hall was built in the second western house after 1360.

A clock and later a bell were put on the tower in the early 15th century. The astronomical clock dates back to this period but a new clock was put on the tower in the early 19th century.

In the mid 15th century the Town Hall was further expanded with the addition of Mikeš the Furrier's house and the complex was renovated in the late Gothic style. An impressive portal was installed in Wolflin's house and a new council hall was built, engraved with the 18 signs of the town councillors. A porch was added at the end of the 15th century, while a richly decorated public hall, with seven windows facing the square, was constructed on the first floor.

In the early 17th century the southern wing was painted with signs and another house was added in 1660. In the late nineteenth century Mikeš house was renovated in the Renaissance style and an assembly hall constructed.

The Minute House, an exquisite building next door, has formed part of the Old Town Hall since 1896. Originally Gothic, it was rebuilt in the second half of the 16th century. The house's facade is decorated with early 17th century sgrafitti of scenes from mythologyand the Bible.

A fire in June 1945 destroyed the eastern wing. The fire also damaged the tower and chapel which were later painstakingly restored.

The astronomical clock is one of Prague's major attractions. The work of 15th century clock-maker Mikuláš of Kadaň, the impressive clock is in two parts. The upper part shows the time, the movement of the sun and moon and the signs of the zodiac, while the lower part shows the months. But it is the hourly ritual marking the passing of time which attracts most attention. The clock chimes, death rings the bells, two windows swing open and the Apostles appear.

The clock was partly destroyed in the 1945 fire while statues of Christ and the Apostles were burnt down and later replaced with copies. The originals of the calendar signs and allegories of the months by J. Mánes which date back to 1865 are now housed in the Prague museum.

Inside on the ground floor are some fine mosaics designed by M. Aleš. On the second floor is a late Renaissance portal leading to the assembly hall decorated with paintings by V. Brožík depicting the Election of George of Poděbrady as King and Jan Huss at the Constance trial. The late Gothic coat of arms of the town and the guilds of Prague are in the old council hall with the pillar ceiling. The wedding hall was last renovated in 1970. Also of interest is the chapel underneath the tower.

The old council hall.

Coat of arms decorating the old council hall.

The twin towers of the Church of Our Lady of Týn.

THE CATHEDRAL OF OUR LADY OF TÝN

With its twin 80 metre high steeples, Týn Church is a major landmark of the Old Town Square, standing in the block between the square and Týnská, Štupartská and Celetná Streets.

The current church, with a triple-nave was built slightly northwest of the former early Gothic church first mentioned in 1135 as a hospice for foreign merchants. Construction began in the mid 14th century, and during the Hussite wars Týn church served as the main Hussite church of Prague. The gable of the main nave was completed in 1463. The northern tower was finished in 1463-1466 while the southern tower was completed in 1506-1511. The church was damaged by fire twice. The vault was rebuilt after a fire in 1679, while the northern tower, burnt down in 1819, was rebuilt in 1835.

The northern portal facing Týnská is graced with a relief of Christ's martyrdom. The original created in Parléř's workshop in 1390 has been replaced with a copy.

The impressive interior with its magnificent array of Baroque furniture was decorated by important painters, among them K. Škréta, J. J. Heinsch. and M. Halbacks and famous sculptors including J. J. Bendl and A. Heidelberger. Of special importance is the early 15th century Gothic Calvary, the Baroque altar (1762-1764), the Gothic tin font (1414), and the Gothic sculpture of the Madonna on a throne (circa 1420).

Also of interest are the sedilia with consoles shaped as heads of the king and queen, the baldachin by M. Rejsek (1493) the early 15th century stone Gothic pulpit and the early Baroque altar with paintings of the Ascension of our Lady and the Holy Trinity by K. Škréta. In the presbytery are two big 16th century canvases by Italian painter G. Romanino. The famous Dutch astronomer at Rudolph II's court, Tycho de Brahe is buried in the church.

The main altar.

Relief of the Baptism of Our Lord, 1649.

The Gothic tin font, 14th century.

The facade of St. Nicholas Church.

View of the dome.

THE CHURCH OF SAINT NICHOLAS

Situated in the northwestern part of the Old Town Square, this imposing church with its Baroque cupola has been rebuilt several times through the centuries.

A church was originally built on this site in the late 13th century. The current church dates back to the 18th century, when architect K. I. Diezenhofer demolished the old church and built a new one with a central nave, presbytery and side chapels. The church was abolished in 1787. Between 1871 to 1920 it served as the Orthodox Church, and in 1920 it became the Hussite Church.

St. Nicholas has a monumental front with a main portal and two towers. The sculptures on the facade are by A. Braun. The frescoes on the cupola vault depicting the lives of St. Nicholas and St. Benedict are by K. D. Asam, who also painted the ceiling paintings in the side chapels and presbytery. The stucco decorations in the interior are by P. Spinetti. The altar was built between 1914-1918. A crystal chandelier from the Harrachov glass works graces the nave.

The main altar.

Detail from the exterior of the Church of St. Jacob.

THE CHURCH OF ST. JACOB
(ST. JAMES)

Situated behind Týn, in Malá Štupartská Street the Church of St. Jacob was built in the Baroque style at the end of the 17th century on the site of an earlier church, founded in 1232 by Wenceslas I and destroyed by fire. It was in the summer refectory of the adjoining monastery that King John of Luxembourg had married his second wife Beatrice in 1337.

The impressive decorations in the interior were completed between 1736-1739. The altar which dates back to 1739 is graced with statues by Schönherr and V.V. Reiner's painting Torture of St. Jacob. A late Gothic sculpture of Pieta, saved from the fire of 1689 has been placed on the altar table. In the left hand nave is the sepulchre of J. V. Vratislav of Mitrovice, the supreme Czech chancellor, designed by Vienna architect J.B. Fischer and decorated with sculptures by F. M. Brokof in 1714-1716. Other important works in the church are by such notable sculptors as F. I. Platzer and J. Wielgus and such painters as I. Voget (who created the ceiling painting from the life of Our Lady and the Holy Trinity) and P. Brandl. The organ dates back to 1705.

Three views of the Convent of St. Agnes.

THE CONVENT OF ST. AGNES

Founded by King Wenceslas I in 1233-34 for the Order of the Poor Clares at the request his sister Anne who became its first abbess, the convent is one of the most important examples of Gothic architecture in Bohemia.

Deserted during the Hussite Wars the convent was taken over by the Dominican Order (1556 to 1626). It was then returned to the Poor Clares until its abolition in 1782 and fell into ruins. Restoration work began in 1892 and was resumed in the 20th century. Since 1963 the complex has housed an exhibition of Czech paintings.

The complex includes the Churches of St. Francis, and St. Saviour, the Chapels of Mary Magdalene and St. Barbara and the Minorite Monastery nearby.

The Chapel of St. Barbara, built in the Gothic style in the late 14th century adjoins the southern wall. On the southern side of the Church of St. Francis is a portal from around 1380 which led to the late 13th century Minorite Monastery.

The monastery church of St. Saviour, built in the mid 13th century, and the two floor Chapel of Mary Magdalene adjoin the presbytery of St. Francis. Entrance is through a triumphal arch, with two capitals decorated with sculptures. The presbytery of the Church of St. Saviour (1270-1280) is one of the first examples of French Gothic art in Bohemia.

Work on the four wing convent of the Poor Clares began in 1233 and continued for a century. The oldest part is the eastern wing, built of bricks with beam ceilings and a dormitory. The refectory dates back to the mid 13th century. Only fragments remain of the northern wing, built in the second half of the 14th century.

The convent houses an important collection by Czech painters including works in the Classic, Empire, Biedermaier and Romantic schools. The former kitchens and refectory now house 19th century art as well as handicrafts, glass, stone, porcelain, cast-iron, tin, textiles and furniture from the Art Industrial Museum of Prague. The Church of St. Saviour, and the presbytery of St. Francis house Czech historical paintings.

Views of the interior of the Powder Tower.

View of the Powder Tower from Celetná Street.

THE POWDER TOWER

The 65 metre high Powder Tower is one of the most important remains of the fortifications of the Old Town. Built between 1475-1483 by M. Václav and M. Rejsek, it takes its name from its use in the 17th century as a storeroom for gunpowder. In 1757 it was damaged by Prussian artillery which destroyed its stone decoration. It was renovated in the neo-Baroque style by J. Mocker more than a century later (1878-1886).

The tower has been associated with all the pomp and circumstance that characterised the coronation processions which started here and wound their way to the Old Town, over Charles Bridge and into the Castle. Two rooms at different levels in the tower house temporary exhibitions. There is a magnificent view of Prague from the top of the tower (180 steps up).

JOSEFOV -- THE JEWISH TOWN

The earliest traces of Jews in Prague date to the tenth century when they settled below the Castle. Their first communities were in the Malá Strana and in Vyšehrad, but these disappeared without trace apparently victims of the First Crusade at the end of the 11th century.

In the 12th century a Jewish community settled north of the market square, now the Old Town Square, and built a synagogue. As the population grew a new synagogue, the Old-New (Staronová) Synagogue, was built in the 13th century. In 1254 Přemysl Otakar II gave privileges to Prague Jews allowing them to practise trade and finance, but they had to pay high taxes. Their quarter was separated by gates and walls from the Christian Old Town. The Jewish community flourished and by the close of the sixteenth century there were more than 12,000 Jews in Prague. This new community gave rise to the Jewish Town.

In 1850 Josefov became a quarter of Prague and the Jews gained citizens' rights. It was named Josefov in honour of Emperor Joseph II. The original housing was demolished during the clearing of the quarter at the turn of 19th century and new buildings were constructed. Today only the Town Hall, six synagogues and the cemetery remain from the original Josefov. The synagogues now form part of the Jewish Museum.

The oldest of the synagogues is the Old-New Synagogue (Staronová Synagogue) in Červená Street which dates to the 13th century. It is one of the first Gothic buildings of Prague and the oldest surviving synagogue in Europe. The Old-New Synagogue is a typical example of a medieval two nave synagogue with a five-cross vault and two eight-sided pillars. The building has richly decorated consoles and a tympanum. Separate areas for women worshippers were added in the 17th and 18th centuries.

Opposite the Old-New Synagogue is the High Synagogue, which was built in 1568 and enlarged in

The Jewish Town Hall.

General view of the Old-New Synagogue and the Jewish Town Hall.

1693. The vault in the interior is decorated in the Renaissance style. Today it exhibits Jewish arts and crafts. Next to the High Synagogue is the Jewish Town Hall capped by a clock tower. Below the clock tower is another clock with Hebrew numerals denoting the hours. Like Hebrew writing, the hands go backwards.

The Pinkas Synagogue on Široká Street, whose walls are inscribed with the names of 77,297 Nazi victims, is a late Gothic building built in 1535 and extended between 1607-1625. The interior is decorated in the Renaissance style.

The Spanish Synagogue was built in 1868 in the Moorish style on the site of an older synagogue. It has a square ground plan with a high cupola and impressive decorations.

Next to the Old Jewish Cemetery is the Klaus Synagogue, built in 1694 on the site of an older synagogue. Next to it is the former ceremonial hall which houses the collection of children's drawings from the Terezín concentration camp .

The Maisel Synagogue was built in 1590-92 as the private synagogue of the Maisel family in the Renaissance style and reconstructed in the neo-Gothic style in the late nineteenth century.

Two views of the Old Jewish Cemetery.

Two views of the interior of the Old-New Synagogue.

The Old Jewish Cemetery was founded in the 15th century and contains several Gothic gravestones which were transferred from older Jewish cemeteries. It is one of the most notable Jewish burial grounds in the world. The oldest gravestone is that of Rabbi Avigdor Karo of 1439 and the most recent that of Moses Beck of 1787 when burials in the cemetery ceased. There are about 12,000 gravestones in the cemetery including that of Rabbi Jehuda Löw ben Bezalel, who created the legendary golem. According to Jewish folklore Löw created the golem out of mud and clay in order to protect the community but one day the golem went on the rampage before dissolving again into mud.

The new Town Hall in Staré Město.

The Municipal Hall.

View of the Clementinum.

Two views of Charles Street.

Two views of Celetná Street.

A riverside view of the Old Town.

The Smetana Museum.

The Smetana Museum.

The statue of Charles IV
in Křížovnické Square.

View of the Vltava from the Old Town.

View of Charles Square.

NOVÉ MĚSTO - THE NEW TOWN AND ITS ENVIRONS

Founded by Charles IV in 1348 the New Town had three markets: the horse market, cattle market and hay market. These are now the site of the three main squares, Wenceslas, Charles and Senovážné.

Named after Bohemia's patron saint, Wenceslas Square is a bustling commercial and shopping centre. In the upper part of the square is the National Museum, dominating the main avenue which leads to the Troja Chateau to the north and the Brno highway to the south.

Opposite the National Museum is the Federal Assembly. Two other notable buildings in the area are the Smetana Theatre, a richly decorated neo-Renaissance building built between 1886-1887 and the Main Railway Station. The station was built at the beginning of the 20th century in the late 19th century decorative style with a cupola hall and a clock tower.

At the lower end of Wenceslas Square is Na Příkopě (On the Moat) Street. Now a busy pedestrian street, Na Příkopě once divided the Old and New Towns. To the south west it leads to Národní (National) Avenue and on to the banks of the Vltava. The National Avenue was built over the original moat, filled up in 1781, and was once one of Prague's most famous promenades. Worth mentioning along this route are the Church of Our Lady of the Snows on Jungmannovo Square and Adria Palace, built between 1923-1925 on Jungmannová Street. Founded by Charles IV in 1347, Our Lady of the Snows was an important Hussite church. Its altar dating back to 1649-1651 is one of the largest in Prague. The Baroque St. Ursula's Church and former convent is also situated on National Avenue.

At the Vltava end of the National Avenue is the National Theatre, a prize example of 19th century Czech architecture. The building was completed in 1881 but was badly destroyed by fire the same year. Work started anew and some of Czechoslovakia's leading artists of the time, such as A. Wagner, A. Liebscher, F. Ženíšek

The Church of the Divine Heart of Our Lord.

Originally a cattle market, Charles Square is the largest square in Prague. It covers an area of 80,550 square metres and is the site of the New Town Hall, Faust's House, St. Ignatius Church, the Czech Technical School and the regional district court.

The New Town Hall, scene of Prague's first defenestration in 1419, was built in the mid 14th century and has been subject to several renovations through the centuries. Faust House, dating back to the same period, was rebuilt several times. Originally a palace, in the 16th century it came into the hands of two famous alchemists associated with Rudolph's court, J. E. Kelley and F. A. Mladota. The house takes its name from popular rumour that they conducted dangerous experiments there. The Church of St. Ignatius was built by C. Lurago between 1658-1670 in the early Baroque style and features some Rococo decorations.

From the southern end of Charles Square, Vyšehradská Street leads to the Church of St. John of Nepomuk, designed in the Baroque style by K. Dientzenhofer in the 1730s and the former Emmaus Monastery. Situated in Ke Karlovu Street a few blocks to the east of Charles Square is the Villa Amerika, designed by the K. Dientzenhofer in the early 18th century. It now houses the Antonín Dvořak Museum.

Back to the lower end of St. Wenceslas Square Na Příkopě Street to the north west leads to Republic Square past the Powder Tower and the Cultural Centre. Two roads lead off from the Powder Tower: Celetná Street a pedestrian walkway leading to the Old Town Hall Square, and Hybernská Street leading to Senovážná Street and Square.

Revoluční Street connects Republic Square with the river. A right turn along Revoluční Street leads to Klimentská Street named after one of Prague's oldest churches, St. Clement (1226-1232). From the church, Nové mlýny (New Mill) Street, leads to the Vltava. It takes its name from the mills that used to stand on the river but only the 17th century water tower survives today.

The Museum of the City of Prague, situated in Šverma Park, can be reached from Klimentská Street.

and M. Aleš, known as the National Theatre generation, assisted in the decoration. The National Theatre was renovated between 1977 and 1983 and a modern building, the New Stage, was built next to it.

Along the embankment from the National Theatre a bridge leads to the picturesque Slavonic Island, a small park in the river Vltava. Further south is Jiráskovo Square. The embankment continues to Vyšehrad, while a turn to the right from the Square leads to Resslova Street, site of the Orthodox Church of Sts Cyril and Methodius. The street connects the embankment with Charles Square.

The National Theatre.

The Main Railway Station.

The equestrian statue of St. Wenceslas.

General view of Wenceslas Square.

WENCESLAS SQUARE

Built by Charles IV in 1348 as a horse market for the New Town, the square, 682 metres long and 60 metres wide, is now a bustling boulevard of shops, office complexes and hotels. It takes its name from the patron saint of Bohemia and is cherished as the venue of some of the country's most dramatic historical events, being inextricably linked with the 1848 revolution, the declaration of an independent state in 1918, the Prague Spring and more recently with the demonstrations which led to the Velvet Revolution.

The imposing building of the National Museum towers over the upper part of the square. But it is the equestrian statue of St. Wenceslas built between 1911 and 1913 by J. V. Myslbek, which is most immediately associated with the square which took his name in 1848. St. Wenceslas

Details of three buildings in Wenceslas Square.

is surrounded by statues of St. Procopius, St. Adalbert, St. Ludmilla and St. Agnes and in the aftermath of the Velvet Revolution has served as a shrine to democracy.

Most of the buildings surrounding the square have been rebuilt. One interesting example of the Czech late 19th century style is the Europa hotel. On the corner with Jindřišská Street and the square is a neo-Baroque palace designed by P. Ohmann and O. Polívka and decorated with reliefs by J. Sucharda, B. Schnirch, C. Vosmík and others. Opposite is the Lucerna Palace, the first reinforced concrete structure in Prague, built by architect Václav Havel in 1913-17. Adjoining it is Melantrich's Palace, built by B. Bendelmayer in 1911-12. On the corner with Vodičkova Street and Wenceslas Square is Wiehls House, (1896-1898).

On the lower end of the square is the Crown Palace built between 1911-1914 with reliefs by S. Sucharda and J. Štursa. The frescoes are by V. Foerster.

The imposing dome of the National Musuem.

The facade of the National Museum.

THE NATIONAL MUSEUM

Built in 1885-1890 the National Museum is one of the oldest and biggest in the country. This monumental building, with its 100 metre long facade and imposing 70 metre high dome towers over the upper part of Wenceslas Square.

The facade is richly decorated with statues and relief panels by such artists as A. Wagner, J. Maudr and F. Hergessel. Themes include Czech history and science. Among the statues on the facade are allegorical figures of the sciences, the virtues and the four elements, while the names of outstanding Czech personalities are inscribed on marble panels.

Inside, the monumental staircase with arcade galleries and the Pantheon with sculptures of national

The monumental staircase and arcade galleries.

View of the Pantheon.

personalities take pride of place. The sculpture decoration of the hall and staircase are by J. S. Schwanthaler, A. Popp and B. Schnirch. Also of interest are wall paintings by J. Mařák and F. Ženíšek among others.

The National Museum as an institution was founded by Kašpar Štarnberk in 1818 and was moved here on the completion of the building. Exhibits cover mineralogy, zoology, paleontology, numismatology and historical and archaeological finds. The museum also houses a large library.

The Grand Hall decorated with wall paintings dating back to the end of the 17th century.

The facade of Troja Chateau.

TROJA CHATEAU

On the outskirts of Prague, opposite the Zoo is Troja Chateau, designed as a summer palace for Count Šternberk by J. B. Matthey and built in 1679-1685.

Set in a well laid out garden and orchard featuring also the Šternberk star, the three-wing building is considered to be one of the finest examples of Czech Baroque architecture. Its most striking characteristic are the magnificent wall paintings which grace the interior.

Troja Chateau now serves as the Municipal Art Gallery of Prague following the completion in 1989 of an ambitious 12 year renovation project.

The central part, including the Grand Hall is one floor higher than the rest of the building. The outstanding wall paintings in the Grand Hall are by Abraham Godyn. Of special importance are the Triumph of Emperor Leopold and the Triumph of Christendom over the Sublime Porte.

Other rooms are decorated with mural paintings of Chinese landscapes while the chapel features a cycle of oil paintings on the life of Jesus by F. Marchetti.

The collection of the Municipal Art Gallery includes 19th century Czech paintings and a smaller section of Baroque paintings.

Outside, the monumental garden staircase is decorated with sculptures of Titans thrown to the underworld by Zeus, the work of J.J. and P. Heerman. The terracotta vases on the terrace are of special importance.

Views of the interior of Troja Chateau.

The Church of Sts. Peter and Paul.

Leopold's Gate.

VYŠEHRAD

Vyšehrad, the fortified former royal seat is built on a promontory overlooking the river Vltava. Its walls encircle several fine churches, an artists' cemetery and a park.

According to the legend it was here that Princess Libuše founded a magnificent palace and foresaw a great future for Prague. Historical evidence, and most notably the denars dating back to 992-1012 produced in the Vyšehrad mint, shows that the area was settled by Slavs in the first half of the 10th century.

Vyšehrad's importance has fluctuated through the centuries, while its tumultuous history and numerous reconstructions have left a mark on the buildings. A royal seat under Vratislav II (1061-1092), Vyšehrad's political significance diminished when the royal seat was moved back across the river to Hradčany. The area came back into the limelight under Charles IV who made it the starting point of the ceremonial coronation processions.

Despite its impregnable position and fortifications Vyšehrad changed hands several times. In 1420 it was taken by the Hussites and 28 years later captured by

General view
of Vyšehrad.

St. Martin's Rotunda.

George of Poděbrady. The fortifications were damaged by the Swedes in 1648 prompting ambitious plans to turn Vyšehrad into an army fortress. Yet less than a century later, Vyšehrad was occupied by the Prussians and in 1866 ceased being a fortress altogether. In 1884 it was incorporated into Prague as its sixth district.

From Vratislova Street entrance to Vyšehrad is through the New or Brick Gate which leads to V. Pevnosti Street.

To the left is the Chapel of Our Lady of the Walls, built in the Baroque style in the 18th century and reconstructed in the neo-Renaissance style in 1882.

Behind it is the Church of St. John the Beheaded, dating back to the second half of the 14th century. Further along, just off the road is the Rotunda of St. Martin. Built towards the end of the 11th century, the rotunda is the only remaining early medieval building in Vyšehrad and during the Thirty Year's War was used to store gunpowder.

The heart of Vyšehrad is the imposing church of Sts. Peter and Paul, founded as a triple nave basilica with a royal crypt by Prince Vratislav II in about 1070 but reconstructed several times through the centuries, most recently in the late 19th and early 20th century during which it took on its current neo-Gothic appearance.

Inside the church is the royal crypt, where Vratislav II, his third wife Svatava, Konrád, Soběslav I and Soběslav II are buried. In the first chapel to the right of the entrance is the Romanesque coffin of St. Longinus, believed to have been the coffin of one of the Přemyslid princes. The only remnants of the Baroque period are wood carved frames and canon pews. The Chapel of Our Lady has a magnificent Gothic panel painting of Our Lady of Vyšehrad, also called Our Lady of the Rains dating back to the first quarter of the 14th century. In the northern nave over the entrance to the sacristy is a painting representing Vyšehrad before it was destroyed in 1420. In the sacristy are 38 paintings of deans and dignitaries.

Nearby is the cemetery, final resting place of hundreds of personalities of the arts and letters. The idea of establishing a national cemetery originates with the Czech Writers' Association towards the end of the 19th century. Part of the cemetery is the Slavín, a common tomb for 50 personalities of the arts built in 1889-93. Another 600 personalities, including composers A. Dvořák and B. Smetana and writers J. Neruda and K. H. Mácha are interred in the cemetery which is graced by a gallery of funeral ornamental sculpture.

Close by in the park are the remains of the medieval palace, three buildings of which have been restored. There is also a 14th century tower, originally part of the fortifications, which now serves as a museum, and remains of a Romanesque bridge dating back to the last quarter of the 11th century. Also of interest are: Libuše's Baths, the old deanery dating back to 1754 and the remains of the Romanesque basilica of St. Vavřinec (St. Lawrence) of the late 11th century. The masonry of the north and cross naves have been preserved while the relief paving stones are the oldest discovered in the western Slav region.

Among the statues in the park is an equestrian statue of St. Wenceslas brought here from Wenceslas Square dating back to 1678.

Back on K Rotunda Street is Leopold Gate designed by Lurago around 1670. The road leads on to the remains of Špička Gate, part of the original fortifications carried out under Charles IV and on to Tábor or Upper Gate built in 1655. Its facade is decorated with Tuscan half columns and embrasures built in the late Renaissance style.

AROUND PRAGUE

Prague not only offers a treasure trove of monuments but serves as a convenient starting off point for day excursions to several historic towns and castles which bring to life the grandeur of medieval Bohemia and boast some magnificent collections of art and weapons. These are set in lush countryside, criss-crossed by rivers and streams and interspersed with numerous small lakes.

Situated some 30 kilometres north of Prague is the town of Mělník, its 14th century castle dominating the river.

Kutná Hora, Bohemia's second most important town in the Middle Ages, is situated 65 kilometres south east of the capital.

About 35 kilometres west of Kutná Hora, close to the Prague-Brno highway, is the Sázava monastery. To the south, dominating the Sázava river, is the castle of Český Šternberk.

Founded in the first half of the 13th century by Zdislav of Divišov, ancestor of the Šternberks, the castle had an eventful history. It was heavily damaged in 1467 when it was administered by an opponent of King George of Poděbrady and was later rebuilt in the late Gothic style. In 1627 the castle was plundered by peasants and in 1648 fell victim to Swedish raids. After the Thirty Years' War it was reconstructed in the early Baroque style. The castle houses an interesting collection of furniture and weapons.

Another magnificent castle is Konopiště. Situated 44 kilometres south of Prague, it houses a rich collection of weapons.

Lake Slapy nearby is ideal for day excursions. Combining a scenic setting with facilities for water sports it is as popular with citizens of Prague as with tourists. The artificial lake, created by the construction of a dam, is 40 kilometres long and surrounded by forested mountains. With opportunities for sailing, fishing and swimming, Slapy serves as a substitute for a sea.

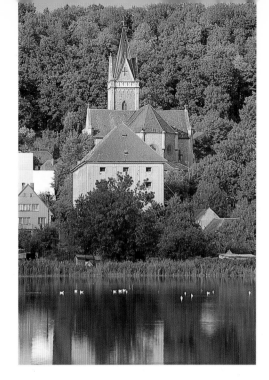

Country scene south of Prague.

From Konopiště the road continues south to Tábor, the town of the Hussites with Lake Jordan, situated 88 kilometres from Prague. Further south is Hluboká Castle on the Vltava, one of Bohemia's most impressive castles.

Built in an impregnable position southwest of Prague is Karlštejn, among the best known of Bohemia's numerous castles. To the northwest of Karlštejn, situated some 35 kilometres from Prague, is Křivoklát Castle.

Overlooking the river, Křivoklát used to be a hunting retreat for Czech princes and kings and was first mentioned in 1109 as a wooden castle.

A stone castle was constructed in the middle of the 13th century, and was extended and fortified towards the end of the 14th century. Gothic reconstruction also commenced at this time and was completed in 1522. The castle was restored in the last quarter of the 19th century through to the 1920s by architect J. Mocker who also built the northern wing.

With its 32 metre high tower the castle boasts an interesting chapel with a late Gothic altar and a library. Exhibits include late Gothic sculptures and paintings.

View from Karlštejn Castle.

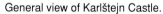
General view of Karlštejn Castle.

KARLŠTEJN

Situated 28 kilometres southwest of Prague this fortress castle was built by Holy Roman Emperor Charles IV in an impregnable location from 1348 to 1357 to house the imperial and Bohemian crown jewels.

Now one of the most famous castles in Czechoslovakia, during the Hussite Wars Karlštejn came under siege in 1422 by the citizens of Prague. It was repaired at the end of the 15th and again in the 16th centuries, but was damaged by Swedish troops in 1648. In the late 19th century the castle was restored in the Gothic style.

In the huge main tower is the Chapel of the Holy Cross decorated with precious and semi-precious stones and paintings of the saints. The Chapel of Our Lady and Chapel of St. Catherine have valuable frescoes and paintings including paintings of Charles IV who used the Chapel of St. Catherine as his private retreat. The Imperial Palace where Charles often stayed is now a museum, and a large part of the collection is dedicated to him.

Views of the fortifications of Karlštejn Castle.

Charles' Room.

St. Catherine's Chapel.

The Church of the Virgin Mary.

Views of Konopiště Castle.

KONOPIŠTĚ

Built in the 14th century by the House of Benešov along the lines of a French chateau with seven circular towers, Konopiště is situated 44 kilometres south of Prague. It was rebuilt in the Gothic style in the beginning of the 16th century by the Šternberks. A century later it was taken over by the Hodějovskýs. In the 18th century it came into the possession of the Count of Vrtba who had the castle redecorated in the Baroque style adding a Baroque gate designed by L. M. Kaňka and sculptures by M. B. Braun. Towards the end of the 19th century the castle was taken over by Archduke Franz Ferdinand who restored Konopiště. A library wing was added in 1914. The castle has an important collection of weapons and hunting trophies and is surrounded by a beautiful park.

Views of the interior of Konopiště including the armoury.

View of the Church of St. Barbara.

KUTNÁ HORA

Situated about 65 kilometres southeast of Prague, Kutná Hora still bears witness to a glorious medieval past which saw it rising to become the second most important town in Bohemia.

Founded in the 13th century, Kutná Hora owes its fame and wealth to the silver deposits which made Czech kings among the richest in Europe and led to the establishment of a royal mint which produced the groš, one of the most valuable and widely used currencies in Europe at the time. But as the silver deposits were exhausted the town gradually lost its importance. With the closing of the mint in 1726 it was relegated to a provincial town.

A major landmark is the Gothic Cathedral of St. Barbara which towers over the town. Construction began towards the end of the 14th century. The

The facade of the Church of St Barbara.

The interior of the Church
of St. Barbara.

The plague column.

The facade of the Stone House.

presbytery was vaulted by M. Rejsek in 1489-1499 while the nave was vaulted by B. Ried in 1512 -1547. The church was reconstructed in 1884-1903. The interior houses some valuable wall paintings from the 15th century and Gothic and Baroque furnishings. Dedicated to the patron saint of miners, the frescoes show miners at work.

Other churches in the town is the parish church of St. Jacob the Greater with its 82 metre high steeple, built between 1320 and 1420 and the Church of Our Lady Mary, built at the end of the 14th century but rebuilt between 1470-1512. The cemetery church of the Holy

Trinity dates back to before 1420 while the Church of St. John Nepomuk, designed by F. M. Kaňka was built between 1734-1750.

One of the most impressive houses in the town, is the Stone House, built in 1480 with a magnificent stone-worked facade and an oriel window.

Vlašský or Italian Court, originally a mint and a royal palace, was founded around 1400 and includes a chapel. Its magnificent interior is open to the public. The Little Castle (Hrádek) was built before 1420 but was reconstructed between 1485-1504. Of special interest is the late Gothic stone well .

The Stone Well.

The Italian Court.

General view of Mělník.

MĚLNÍK

The hill town of Mělník, surrounded by vineyards controls the confluence of the rivers Elbe and Vltava. Once a royal town popular with Bohemia's queens, its major landmark is Mělník Castle, dominating the landscape from the top of the hill. The castle was rebuilt in the Gothic style in the second half of the 14th century. It was fortified and rebuilt the following century when a Renaissance wing with arcades was added. Nearby is the Church of Sts. Peter and Paul originally Romanesque with a well preserved crypt rebuilt in the 1480s. The tower and triple nave date back to that period. The council house is of Gothic origin. It was rebuilt between 1765-1792 and the last adaptation was carried out 1939-141. Viticulture in the area owes much to Emperor Charles IV who introduced vines from Burgundy.

View from Mělník.   Views of Mělník.

General view of Tábor and Lake Jordan.

TÁBOR

Founded in the early 15th century on the site of a former medieval castle situated 88 kilometres south of Prague, Tábor was closely associated with the Hussites who made the town their headquarters and called it after Mount Tábor in Galilee.

Parts of the fortifications and many late Gothic and Renaissance houses from the 15th century have been proudly preserved to this day. The lay-out of the streets, and the web of tunnels below the square bear witness to the military concerns of the Hussites. The town square called Žižkovo after Jan Žižka, the Hussite military chief is the site of the Old Gothic town hall built in the 15th century and the Gothic church (1440-1512) with Renaissance gables dating back to 1550. The remains of the 14th century castle with a well preserved tower and Kotnovská gate are also worth visiting. On the edge of Tábor is the artificial lake of Jordan, created in 1492 and used by the Hussites for baptisms.

View of Tábor's main square.

Views of the Castle of Hluboká.

THE CASTLE OF HLUBOKÁ ON THE VLTAVA

With its battlements and turrets, dominating the Vltava river and the town of Hluboká, it is one of the most impressive castles in the country. Built originally as a Gothic castle in the second half of the 13th century it was rebuilt as a Renaissance castle for the Lords of Hradec in the end of the 16th century.

The Schwarzenberks turned it into a Baroque castle (1721-1728).In the 19th century extensive reconstruction gave the 140-room castle its current Romantic-Gothic appearance. Inside the richly decorated interiors the castle houses fine collections of furniture and weapons. The stables have been converted into a gallery and house the Aleš South Bohemian gallery.

Sázava Monastery.

Křivoklát Castle.

Český Šternberk Castle.

Views of Lake Slappy.

CONTENTS

AKNOWLEDGEMENTS:

Our thanks are due to:
The authorities and staff of Prague Castle, the Loreto, Strahov Monastery, Museums and Art Galler ies, the Old Town Hall, the Jewish Museum, Troja Chateau, Konopiště Castle and Karlštejn Castle for permission to photograph antiquities, religious and art objects and assisting us with the photography. To Mrs Anna-Rita Baglioni for preparing the Italian translation, Miss Marina Adamides for preparing the French translation and Mr Werner Müller for preparing the German translation of this edition. To Mrs J Leonidou, Mrs H Georgiou, Mrs E Solomonidou, Mrs R Repond, Mrs R Hadjioannou, Mr G Stromberger, Mr D Rath, Mr J Jeřábek, Mr J Kopřiva and Mr A Coutas for their valuable contribution in the preparation of this edition.
Special thanks are due to Mrs S Rathova and Mr J Žůrek of K.P.M.G Prague, Mrs Ch Barnett and Dr J Svoboda.

PUBLISHED BY:
Ghinis Publishing Limited,
13 Stassinou Avenue,
P.O.Box 1329,
Nicosia,
CYPRUS

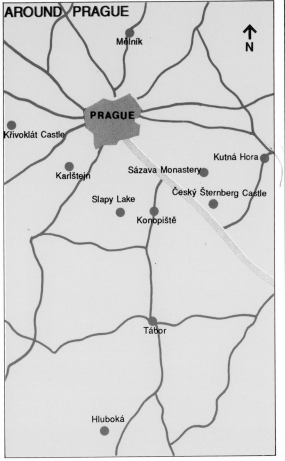

AROUND PRAGUE

N

Mělník
PRAGUE
Křivoklát Castle
Karlštejn
Slapy Lake
Sázava Monastery
Kutná Hora
Český Šternberg Castle
Konopiště
Tábor
Hluboká

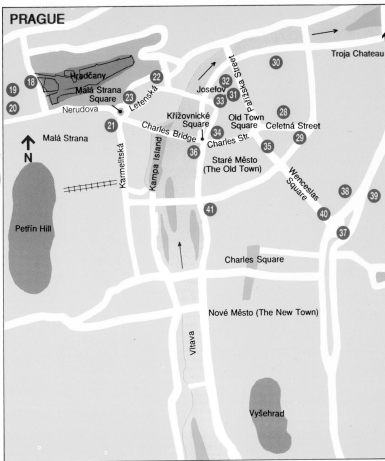

PRAGUE

Troja Chateau
Hradčany
Malá Strana Square
Nerudova
Malá Strana
N
Petřín Hill
Josefov
Křížovnické Square
Charles Bridge
Kampa Island
Karmelitská
Letenská
Old Town Square
Pařížska Street
Celetná Street
Charles Str.
Staré Město (The Old Town)
Wenceslas Square
Charles Square
Nové Město (The New Town)
Vltava
Vyšehrad

19) 18) 20) 22) 23) 21) 30) 32) 31) 33) 28) 34) 36) 35) 29) 38) 39) 41) 40) 37)

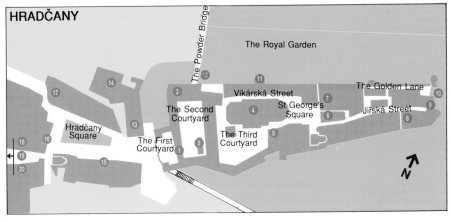

HRADČANY

The Powder Bridge
The Royal Garden
Vikárská Street
The Golden Lane
The Second Courtyard
St George's Square
Jiřská Street
Hradčany Square
The First Courtyard
The Third Courtyard
N

14) 12) 11) 17) 3) 10) 13) 4) 7) 9) 16) 2) 5) 6) 8) 18) 1) 19) 15) 20)

THE OLD TOWN SQUARE

N

26) 27) 25) 24)

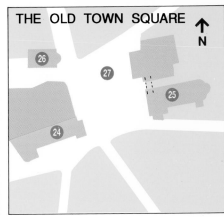

1) The Matthias Gate
2) The Holy Cross Chapel
3) The Castle Picture Gallery
4) St. Vitus Cathedral
5) The Royal Palace
6) St. George's Basilica
7) The Convent of St. George-Bohemian Art Gallery
8) Lobkowicz Palace
9) The Eastern Gate
10) The Black Tower
11) The White Tower (Bihulka)
12) The Northern Gate
13) The Archbishop's Palace
14) Šternberk Palace-Collection of European Art
15) Schwarzenberk Palace-Museum of Military History
16) Tuscany Palace
17) Martinic Palace
18) The Loreto
19) Černin Palace
20) Strahov Monastery
21) The Church of St. Nicholas
22) Wallestein Gardens
23) St. Thomas Church
24) The Old Town Hall
25) Týn Cathedral
26) The Church of St. Nicholas
27) The statue of John Huss
28) The Church of St. Jacob
29) The Powder Tower
30) The Convent of St. Agnes
31) The Jewish Town Hall
32) The Old-New Synagogue
33) The Jewish cemetery
34) The Clementinum
35) Tyl Theatre
36) Smetana Museum
37) The National Museum
38) Smetana Theatre
39) The Main Railway Station
40) The statue of St. Wenceslas
41) The National Theatre

This edition was printed at Proodos printing
works Nicosia, Cyprus. Colour separations
by Bastas-Plessas Athens, Greece.
Computer work for texts by Chr. Andreou Ltd
Nicosia, Cyprus. Artistic supervision by
Mr. George Simonis.